BRAINS

AND

HOW TO GET THEM

BY

CHRISTIAN D. LARSON

Author of

"The Ideal Made Real," "The Hidden Secret," "On the
Heights," "The Pathway of Roses," "The Great
Within," "How to Stay Young," "Mastery
of Fate," "How the Mind Works,"
"Your Forces and How to
Use Them,"
Etc.

CONTENTS

PAGE

Introduction:—New Discoveries in Brain Building 5

CHAPTER

    I. Building the Brain............... 31
    II. Making Every Brain Cell Alive.... 46
    III. Principles in Brain Building....... 55
    IV. Practical Methods in Brain Building 71
    V. Vital Secrets in Brain Building.... 89
    VI. Special Brain Development........124
    VII. The Inner Secret 135
    VIII. The Finer Forces 142
    IX.. Subjective Concentration 146
    X. Principle of Concentration.......151
    XI. Development of Business Ability...159
    XII. Accumulation and Increase.......164
    XIII. Individual Advancement 170
    XIV. The Genius of Invention..........176
    XV. The Musical Prodigy 189
    XVI. Talent and Genius in Art.........208
    XVII. Talent and Genius in Literature....218

Conclusion:—Vital Essentials in Brain Building 225

INTRODUCTION

NEW DISCOVERIES IN BRAIN BUILDING

When we consider the human brain, together with mental brilliancy, mental power and mental capacity, we find three factors in particular that stand out distinctly; and we also find that the more we have of these three factors, the more brains we possess.

The first factor is the physical cells of the brain; the second factor is the quality of the mind acting through the brain; and the third factor is the actions of the mind itself.

The actions of the mind we may also speak of as mental force; that is, that power in the mind that is distinct both from mental quality and the physical side of the brain; and we always find that the possession of an exceptional degree of this mental force or power, always means mental brilliancy as well as high mental activity.

The fact that these three factors, when highly developed, invariably produce a greater quantity and a higher degree of brains, leads us to inquire how the further development of these factors may be promoted; and we now know that these factors can be developed.

In the past we lived largely in the belief that the increase of talent or ability was something that we might not expect—something that was hardly possible in any case; and therefore we felt it necessary to be content with what ability we might happen to be born with. This however, we do not believe any more, because any number of intensely interesting experiments conducted along these lines have proven conclusively that brains can be developed.

This same fact is being proven every day by a great number of individuals who are constantly building up the mind and its power, through the best methods that they have been able to find in modern psychology. We have all noted how certain people have improved during certain periods of time when they gave attention to the newest principles of mind development; and in many cases such improvement has been remarkable. We may therefore proceed in the conviction that brains can be developed, and that an individual can develop his own brains, not only to a certain degree, but to any degree desired.

Considering the first factor—the cells of the brain—we come face to face with a very interesting fact that has been evolved in recent years through certain laboratory experiments, and this fact is, that the cells of the brain can be increased in number and improved in quality through the mere act of increasing life and power in the various groups of the brain cells. To illustrate, we will suppose that you divide your brain into five or six divisions, and take, say, one-half hour, twice every day, for the purpose of concentrating attention upon those various divisions, for the express purpose of increasing life and energy throughout the brain; you will find, in the course of a few weeks' time, that every part of your brain will be more active than it was before; and you will note a remarkable increase in the power and capacity of the mind as a whole. We all are familiar with the fact that whenever we concentrate attention upon any group of cells, either in the body, or in the brain, we invariably increase life, energy, and nourishment among those cells; and the result must be development.

These experiments in concentration prove that the circulation can be increased anywhere in the human system, at the point of concentration; and we know full well that whenever we increase the circulation, we supply added nourishment as well as added life force. We understand therefore, that by providing the different divisions of the brain with added nourishment and life force, through this process of concentration, we provide those very essentials that nature requires in order to build more cells, as well as develop further the cells already existing in that particular group.

This same mode of concentration tends to increase brain activity, and wherever brain activity is increased, there we always find a corresponding improvement in quality, together with finer mental action, deeper mental action, and a more refined mode of mental functioning, which invariably leads to superior thinking.

The development of the brain through this method does not necessarily mean an enlargement of the brain on the whole, for the fact is that the higher development of the brain tends to produce more cells and smaller cells, so that where one crude cell might have existed before, we may produce a dozen or more finer cells; and the law is, that the finer the cells of the brain, the more perfect the brain becomes as an instrument through which ability, talent and genius may be expressed. However, if this process of brain development is continued for a number of years, the entire cranium will have increased in size to some extent. We find in great men and great women who have used their brains and minds extensively all through life, that the measurement of the cranium has increased slightly every ten years; and in some instances we find that the circumference of the cranium has increased one entire inch after the age of sixty. This fact proves conclusively that brain development may be continued far beyond the half century mark; and that ability may be increased remarkably even after the three score and ten has been passed; in fact, the new psychology is proving conclusively that we can increase ability, talent, brain capacity and mental power every year as long as we live, so that any man may become far more brilliant at the age of one hundred than he might have been at any previous time in his life.

When we consider this process of brain development, and the possibility of increasing the number of cells in the brain, we meet a very interesting fact. We will suppose that a certain group of cells in your brain is composed of just one hundred cells. This means that there would be one hundred points of action through which the mind could act in that particular part of the brain; but if you could double that number of cells you would have two hundred points of action through which the mind could be expressed along that line; and in consequence mental capacity and power would exactly double along that particular line of expression. Then suppose that you would promote your development further, and build twelve small, highly refined cells for every one brain cell you previously had; the capacity of the mind would become just exactly twelve times as great as it was before. You would have twelve times as many channels for the expression of talent and genius as you had previously; and the creative power of your mind would be twelve times as large as it was in the past.

It may not be possible for every brain to increase the number of cells to this extent; but every brain can double and treble its number of cells; and a large number, especially those who are faithful, will find it possible to increase the number of brain cells to eight, ten, and twelve times during the course of several years of steady brain development.

This fact brings us face to face with marvelous possibilities; it proves conclusively that there is no need of any one, at any time, being discouraged on account of a lack of ability or lack of opportunity, because even a few months of development of the brain will bring the individual to a place where he will be able to handle and master problems and propositions that he never could have managed before. Besides, this increase of development of the brain will give added ability and power in proportion and we all know very well that however discouraging the present may be, we shall find it possible to take advantage of new and exceptional opportunities the very moment we can add to our ability and power.

In this connection, we must remember that every cell in the brain serves as a channel for mental action. Therefore, the more cells we have in the brain, the more mental actions there will be; and the increase of mental actions means increase of mental capacity, mental power, and also mental creative force.

Mental action, however, does not depend on size, so that a brain cell does not have to be large in order to serve as a perfect channel for mental action. The fact is that the smaller the brain cell is, the more perfect it becomes as a channel for mental action. Therefore, we see the advantage of securing smaller brain cells and more brain cells; and this we may accomplish through the process of brain development, which we shall here outline.

We find that all such development tends to re-build all the cells of the brain; and in re-building those cells, the brain texture is made finer, and the cells themselves smaller and more numerous. The psychology of all of this is very simple, as we shall find the more deeply we study this important subject.

The study of brain development also proves conclusively that the brain or the mind does not wear out. We had that opinion in the past, but it has been discarded as absolutely untrue. The use of the brain does not, in itself, tend to wear upon the brain, for the fact is, that use should constitute, and does constitute exercise; and the more we exercise any faculty or factor, the greater will be the development of that faculty or factor.

The same is true of experience. We have been in the habit of believing that experience will wear on the human system; but the contrary is the truth. Every experience should increase the power of the mind, and the reason why is simple. Every new experience you pass through, should, and naturally does, lead the mind into a new field. It adds a new dominion to the field of consciousness; and our capacity to apply consciousness must increase accordingly. When consciousness acts in a limited field it is limited; but when that field is enlarged consciousness is enlarged in proportion; and the larger the field of consciousness, the larger, the greater and the more brilliant becomes the mind.

Every new experience, every new line of growth, and every new line of mental activity, will naturally add to the powers and the domains of the mind. Thus we secure a larger mental field, and this is one of our principal objects in view. We should always look upon experience in this way; and if we take this view of experience, we tend to encourage the mind to go farther and farther in the expansion of consciousness, whenever a new experience is entertained or enjoyed. The result will be that every experience will have a tendency to enlarge the mind and add to the field of consciousness.

In building up the cells of the brain, we may consider a few simple methods that have proven themselves most effective through actual experience. This study, however, is very recent, and there are only a few who have undertaken to demonstrate the effectiveness of the principles involved; but we have secured enough facts to substantiate absolutely the science of this new brain development. We may therefore proceed with the full conviction that the results desired will be secured.

The first principle to consider is that of concentration, and the power of concentration to increase life, energy and circulation in any part of the human system where we may choose to concentrate. You can prove this power through various experiments. Concentrate your attention upon your hand, and in a few minutes your hand will become warm. Very soon you will note the veins on the back of the hand beginning to swell, proving conclusively that the circulation there has been increased to a very large extent. Concentrate your attention upon your feet, with a desire to increase the circulation all the way down through your body, and you will soon feel a glowing warmth all over the surface of the skin, and the feet themselves will become quite warm. This method has been found very effective in preventing a cold, in case we should feel such a condition coming on; because it is a well known fact that the increase of the circulation all over the body will tend to open the pores of the skin, and thus enable nature to eliminate those very conditions that are brewing in the system when a cold is threatened.

There are many ailments in the human system that can be prevented or overcome in the same way, because we know very well that the increase of the circulation, with life and energy is all that is necessary to cure a disease, or prevent any ailment, whatever the circumstances may be. We understand therefore that we can, through the process of concentration, increase life, energy and circulation anywhere in the system, and therefore in any group of cells in the brain.

Begin by concentrating attention upon the different parts of the brain; and during the process of concentration try to feel deeply; that is, try to enter into the spirit of this concentration; and express, through your concentration, a very deep desire for the increase of life, energy and action in that group of cells upon which your concentration is directed. It is a positive fact that this method alone will, during a year's time, if practiced every day, increase brain capacity from fifty to three hundred per cent in almost any brain that we might mention.

The mere development of the brain, however, and the cells of the brain, is not all that will follow through this method; for the fact is, that most of us have talents and powers within us that are constantly clamoring for expression, but that cannot find expression, because the brain is not sufficiently developed to act as a proper channel. There are many people in this condition. They feel genius within them, but that genius cannot find expression. They are restless and ambitious, but they do not know what to do with themselves, because the power within them is pent up, so to speak, and is unable to do anything along any definite line. In the minds of these people the brain cells are not attuned to the powers and genius within them, and therefore they accomplish nothing. But if these people would take up this method of concentration upon the brain, they would soon develop the brain sufficiently, and refine the brain sufficiently, to give at least a part of this genius and power within them an opportunity for this expression; and gradually as they continued this development, more and more of the genius within them would find expression, until they would pass from what appeared to be ordinary mental capacity to exceptional genius.

The fact is that there are thousands of people in the world who have exceptional genius within them, but their brains are not fine enough to give this genius an opportunity to come forth and act. All of these people therefore would become highly talented and possessed of genius in actual action, if they would develop their brains; and this simple method of concentration will do far more than we ever dreamed along this particular line.

There are many instances in history where people have been practically of no value mentally, until after forty, fifty or sixty; then suddenly exceptional ability came forth; and this fact can be explained when we know that remarkable genius, if active in the within, will continue to try to express itself and refine the brain, until finally the brain becomes sufficiently developed to give that genius expression; but if we do not assist this genius within, it may take a half a century or more before the brain will, in this indirect way, become fine enough through which genius may act. But we need not wait for this slow and indirect process; in fact, we must not wait; we must proceed at once to build up our brains so that we may give what genius we have full opportunity to work itself out and become a power in life.

In applying this mode of concentration, give a few moments, two or three times every day, to every part of the brain, dividing the brain into

eight or ten divisions; and always concentrate
with deep feeling, and in a calm, gentle attitude;
but be tremendously in earnest.   Try to feel the
finer life and the finer forces of life as you concentrate and try to enter into the very spirit of the
process.   The result will be increased brain and
mental activity in every instance; and as this process of development is continued, brain development will continue until we may succeed in building up the brain with ten or twelve times as many
cells as the brain had before; and also in building
up cells that are highly refined, highly cultivated,
thereby becoming perfect instruments, through
which the highest degree of genius and talent
may find expression.

Another exceptional advantage to be gained,
through this mode of concentration is this, that
the entire brain will come more perfectly under
our control so that whenever we want to change
mental action, we can bring about that change
almost immediately.   We are all familiar with
the fact that the average brain responds very
slowly to any changed line of thought.   It moves
and lives in a groove; and where the individual
may desire to act along another line for a time,
it is almost impossible to do so, because the brain
does not respond to the new field of mental action
selected. In other words, such brains find it necessary to work at about the same thing every day,

and they continue this all through life, a state of affairs which is by no means desirable, as it means a narrow world of nothing beyond mere existence.

However, if we make it a practice to concentrate upon the brain every day, we train the will to gain more and more perfect control of the brain; and we also make the brain itself more responsive to all our desires and intentions. Therefore, whenever we wish to act along another line, or take up some other work, the brain will adapt itself almost immediately to the new demand; and we can proceed with the new line of work with practically no loss of time.   This, we realize is of an immense advantage, for we all come to places, every few days, when we are called upon to consider subjects and problems with which we are not dealing constantly; and if we can direct the brain to respond immediately to this new line of mental action, we can take up those problems at once, and deal with them as if we had been working along that line for years.

In this process of brain development, the principal thing to consider is that of making the entire brain active.   We know that in the average brain, only about one cell out of every ten is active; and even among very fine brains, fully one-half of the cells are almost totally inactive.   Therefore, if we would wake up, so to speak, the whole

brain, and make every cell active, we might in
that way alone, increase mental activity and brain
capacity fully 100 per cent; and in some instances,
to a far greater degree.

Here we find the principal reason why most
minds are so limited in capacity and endurance.
We know that the average mind becomes exhausted very soon and the reason is that the average mind uses only about one-tenth of the cells
of the brain. If the mind could use all the cells
of the brain instead of only one-tenth, we should
have ten times as much brain capacity and endurance as we had before. We realize therefore
the tremendous value of this simple method of
brain concentration; but in all this work, we must
remember that the brain is a very delicate instrument, and responds only to those actions that are
deeply calm and tremendously in earnest. We
must train ourselves therefore, to feel the deeper,
finer mental forces of body, personality and
mind; and we must try to get into constant touch
with those finer elements that are at work in the
deeper subconscious field. Most minds feel this
energy to a considerable extent, and most people
who are ambitious have moments when these
finer energies are felt to the very depth of the
soul; and it is at such moments that ambitious
minds feel as if they could accomplish anything,
and it is certainly true that we can accomplish

anything if we learn to apply all the talent and genius and power that we possess. But we must awaken the deeper, finer and more penetrating forces of mind and soul, because these forces are both limitless and invincible.

For practical purposes, it might be suggested that each individual take five or ten minutes every morning for brain concentration; then five or ten minutes more in the middle of the day; and possibly ten or fifteen minutes in the early part of the evening; but whenever we have three or four minutes at any time of the day, it is a splendid practice to become quiet and turn attention upon various parts of the brain, with a desire to promote the increase of life, energy and power. We should go about this process, however, in a very gradual manner, and always be calm and serene, but *tremendously in earnest*. We should look for results from the very beginning, although we must never permit ourselves to become discouraged, should results fail to appear at once. This system will do the work. It will develop the brain; and all we need do is to persevere to secure the results we desire.

An important fact to remember is, that this mode of brain concentration is not to be used for a short time only. It should be used constantly all through life, because it will not only promote continuous development, but will prevent brain cells from becoming dormant; that is, it will continue to make the whole brain alive; and as long as the whole brain is alive the brain will be young, vigorous, virile and wide awake.

The reason why people lose their memory and their mental brilliancy after they have lived thirty, forty or fifty years, is because they permit so many brain cells to become dormant; but this can be prevented by the simple practice of concentrating upon the entire brain for a few moments every day; and as we proceed with this concentration, we should turn on the full current, and try to increase steadily the natural amount of energy that is generated by the brain and the mind. And one thing is certain, that after we have continued this mode of development for a time, until the brain begins to respond to the will, we shall find a decided increase of power, talent, ability and capacity along every line. We may not notice much increase until the brain begins to respond to the will, and to this process of concentration, but this response will come in a few days or a few weeks to most minds; and after that time most excellent results may be expected in a greater and greater measure.

The second factor is that of quality; and quality consists of any number of elements, the principal ones being mental refinement, high mental activity and complexity of mental activity. To improve the quality, therefore, of the brain and of the mind, the first essential is to refine all our thinking; and the most direct course to pursue in mental refinement is to try to form correct and finer mental conceptions of everything of which we may be thinking.   In other words, we should train ourselves to think towards the ideal side of every circumstance, every condition, every factor and every living entity that we may observe or meet in life; in this manner our thinking will become more and more refined, and the quality of mind and brain will improve accordingly.

Another essential in the improvement of quality is to cause the mind to pass from the simple to the complex in all its mental conceptions. To illustrate: If you are thinking of a certain object and have only one general idea of that object, your thinking at that time is very simple.   But if you try to consider that object from every imaginable point of view, you will find, that instead of forming one idea of the object, you will form a score or more.   Your mental conception therefore of that object will become very large, very extensive and very complex.   That object will give you ten, twenty, fifty or possibly one hundred different ideas, instead of one idea which would be the case if you thought of that object in a general way only, and only along a certain line. It is a most excellent practice to make it a point to try to think of every object or subject from as many viewpoints as possible. This will not only give the mind many new ideas, but it will train the mind to act along many new lines, and in addition will improve the quality of the mind in every form and manner.

An important gain in this connection is that of enjoyment. We all have the privilege to enjoy life in as many ways as possible, provided the enjoyment is wholesome and beneficial; and we shall find that the more complex the mind becomes, that is, the more channels there are in the mind, through which we can think and act, the greater will be our enjoyment of everything that we may entertain in life. We will be able to appreciate an immense universe instead of merely a few elements, as before; and we will begin to live in a world that will contain hundreds and even thousands of times as many interesting states or fields of consciousness as we found in the world in which we lived in the past. In brief, our state of existence will become a harp of a thousand strings instead of merely a harp of a few strings, as is the case with the average person.

Our object should always be to enlarge life, to enlarge consciousness, to enlarge the field of the mind, and to multiply the number of channels through which the mind can find action, because the more lines of expression there are, the more talent and genius we can apply in practical life; and we shall find that the practice of making all thinking more complex, that is, learning to see everything from every imaginable viewpoint, will tend directly to produce this enlargement of the mental field; and results will be numerous as well as highly desirable, in every form and manner.

The study of mental quality is one that is very large and very deep; and it is a subject that will be considered more thoroughly as we proceed in this study; but for practical purposes the above will be sufficient; and we will therefore proceed to the third factor—the increase of the actions of the mind itself.

Every faculty must have a certain amount of energy and life; and to increase the energy and life of each particluar faculty, we must learn, first, that it is what we realize in that faculty that actually finds expression.

We might define the actions of the mind as the inner power of thought, or what might also be called, the *thinking* of the faculty or the talent that is being employed. To illustrate, take the faculty of music. We shall find that it is large, active and brilliant in proportion to how well the musician can really *think* music; and to *think* music, we enter into the spirit of music itself. The mind acts in the world of music, or in the real soul of music instead of simply viewing the element of music from a distance. We shall find it to be a fact, that if we wish to increase mental activity through any talent or faculty, we must *think* that talent, and *think* that talent more and more: and we *think* a talent whenever mind or soul expresses itself through the soul of that talent, forming at the time distinct and definite ideas of the talent itself. Whenever we employ a faculty, we find that a certain force is being expressed through that faculty, and that force consists of *thinking* what is absolutely in that faculty itself.

To illustrate: When you *think* music, you do not think of music, but you really *think* music; and there is a vast difference. You must understand the difference, if you wish to attain genius. When you *think* invention, you do not think of invention, but you *think* invention itself. When you *think* business you do not think of business, but you *think* business itself; that is, you think through the life and spirit of the business faculty in your possession; and when you *think* business, your business faculty is acting, not round about the business element, but is acting through the business element; and is consequently producing definite and valuable business ideas. You will find that when you think business according to this definition, your mind will naturally create better business ideas, better business plans and methods than it has ever done in the past, because you are acting in the business faculty itself, in the very spirit, soul and essence of it, and in that part of the mind that has the power to apply itself in the commercial world.

It will be very evident to the student that it is difficult to define in words, what it is to "think" your talent, or to think a faculty. It is something that we must realize through our own experience; but when we attain this realization we shall find that when we make a special effort to enter *into* a faculty and talent whenever we think of that talent, and at the same time try to *think* what the talent already is and can do, we are getting down to rock bottom in this immense field.

We should proceed therefore to try to *think* the ability or talent we possess, or the ability and talent we wish to develop, whatever that ability may be; and by so doing, we will increase the real vital activity of that ability or talent in itself, and thus enter into that indefinable something in the mind that we speak of as native talent or as native genius. It is indefinable; it is real; it is natural; it is inherent; it is second nature. It is an inseparable part of the mind.

We should also make it a point to think of every talent as a growing talent. Think of your faculties and talents as evolving, developing and creating more power. Picture in your mind every talent as being in a process of building. Think of your consciousness as delving deeper and deeper into this vast interior mental process, where talent and genius are created. Think of your whole mind as becoming more and more alive. We know there is something alive in the mind that we call talent. There is a mental power that comes from the depth of the soul; and when the brain begins to respond to that power from within, that power will work itself out through all the cells of the brain, and the result will be that all those cells will become direct channels for a larger, a greater and a stronger expression of all the ability, talent, power or genius that we may arouse within. It is then that the mind becomes a live wire, so to speak; and when the mind becomes a live wire, we shall have no more dormant brain cells and no more inactive forces in our mental world. Every power, faculty and talent we possess will begin to work, and will work constructively as well as effectively along the lines that we have decided upon. The result will be that capacity, power, ability, talent and genius will increase along all lines; and this increase may be continued steadily and uninterruptedly as long as we live.

We must proceed in the conviction that we not only have the power to arouse all the latent capacity and talent within us, but we also have the power to build up and develop that capacity and talent to any degree desired, and for an indefinite period; and here we should remember that the mind has the faculty of rebuilding itself, again and again, on a larger and a larger scale for any length of time.   The mind that you have today can double its own power and talent during the present year; and next year this mind that has been doubled, can repeat the process and double once more this larger life and capacity that has been gained.   Later, this process can be repeated again and continued indefinitely.

It matters not therefore how small a mind you may have today, you can double the power of that mind again and again as long as you live, until it becomes a prodigious mind, and you become a mental giant.   Remarkable possibilities therefore lie before us in this wonderful study; and those who will persevere in the correct application of these principles, will succeed in making real the ideal of these possibilities, steadily and surely in every direction; so therefore no matter how high our ideals may be, or how difficult the undertakings we have in view, those undertakings can be carried out successfully, and every ideal realized. The power to do those things does exist within us; and whenever we want more power than we have now, we need only remember that every human mind has the faculty of rebuilding itself on a larger scale, again and again, for any length of time.

BRAINS AND HOW TO GET THEM

CHAPTER I

BUILDING THE BRAIN

Function of the Brain—The brain is to the mind what the piano is to the pianist, or what any instrument of expression is to that which is being expressed. To develop the brain, therefore, to the very highest degree is necessary if the mind is to make full application and tangible use of every power that may be latent in the great within of the subconscious. The brain as a whole, as well as every cell in the brain, must become perfectly responsive to every action the mind may make, and must possess the capacity to give that action the full volume of power required. The brain must possess the capacity of much work, and must also possess that fineness of quality that is necessary to the highest order of work. In brief, to supply the demands of genius, the brain as well as the mind must be able to furnish both quantity and quality.

Modern Methods—The methods employed in modern education tend in a measure to develop the brain. The practical use of the mind will develop the brain in parts, but such development is both indirect and inadequate. The average mind is much greater than the brain it is trying to use; therefore, it does not accomplish what it has the power to accomplish. To develop the brain even to a slight degree, would in many instances give the mind almost twice as much active capacity and ability as is possessed now, while if such development were promoted thoroughly and in conjunction with further mental development, there would be a decided increase in ability; and in many instances actual genius would appear. In the average brain there are millions of cells that are practically dormant. They are never called into action, and in consequence serve only as obstacles to the efforts of the mind. In fact, in many brains more than half of the cells are not in use. They are constantly being enriched or reconstructed, but they do not serve the mind in any way; and such brain cells as do not permit the expression of the mind will invariably prevent that expression.

Active Brain Cells—The more active brain cells we possess the more mental power we can express. The mental power and ability that is back of the physical brain is limitless, but the cells of the physical brain are only channels through which talent and genius are coming forth. To increase the number of active brain cells, therefore, is one of the chief essentials in the development of genius. When all the cells that now exist in the brain are made active, the mind, if correspondingly developed, will become exceptional in brilliancy and power. But if the mind should so develop that the present number of cells would not be adequate, the number could be increased without changing the regular size of the brain to any extent, although the brain as a whole always becomes a little larger when high development of both brain and mind is taking place. In the crude brain the cells are large and sluggish. In the developed brain the cells are small, refined and very active. In fact, the smaller the brain cell the better it becomes as an instrument of the mind, the reason being that the more closely the cell approaches a point of action, the more perfect the concentration of mental action; and the more perfect the concentraton of any action, the greater the power and efficiency of that action. When the brain is well developed all the large sluggish cells will be removed, and the space will be filled with an extra number of small active cells; in consequence a well developed brain has several times as many cells as an undeveloped brain, although the size of the two brains may be the same. And since the cells of the well developed brain will all be alive ready to respond to the mind, we can readily see the advantage of thorough brain development.

The Three Essentials—The brain of the genius is always very fine in the quality of its substance; and this is the first essential. The second essential is an increase in the number of active brain cells. In fact, where we feel real genius we find every brain cell thoroughly alive and in a high state of vibration. The third essential is the awakening of the subconscious life of every brain cell. The brain of the genius is very strong on the subconscious side; and this is one reason why such a brain sometimes gives expression to what seems to be super-human attainments. Every cell contains a subjective or subconscious life; that is, an inner life that is far greater in power, capacity and efficiency than any phase of life that may exist merely on the surface; and when this subconscious life is fully alive in all the brain cells, we will naturally have a brain that is inexhaustible in capacity and power.

Necessary Elements—There are a number of elements that go to make up genius. One of these is unlimited capacity for work; and this is secured when the subconscious life and power of every cell in the brain becomes alive. Such a brain will not be used up no matter how complex, how intricate or how extensive the actions of the mind may be. It is equal to every occasion that the mind may meet, no matter how difficult, and it can easily hold out until the task is finished. The average brain is used up after a few hours of full mental action; and the reason is found in the fact that its capacity is limited. In such a brain the deep, inexhaustible subconscious life is not awakened, therefore it has but little to draw upon. In the brain of the genius, however, there is any amount of life and power upon which to draw. Every cell is literally alive with unlimited subconscious life, and therefore no matter how great the demands of the mind may be, the brain is fully equal to all of those demands.

Increased Capacity—When the mind is inspired by great ambitions, the desire to do great things in the world becomes stronger and stronger. In consequence, the mind will attempt to obey these desires; in fact, it will have no peace until it does. But if the brain does not have the power and the capacity to work as much and as long as the mind may require in order to carry out these ambitions, failure will inevitably follow. And here we have one reason why so many important undertakings with every opportunity for remarkable success have failed almost from the beginning. The men behind those undertakings had the ambition and the courage to proceed, but they did not have the brain capacity to hold out, the reason being that their brain cells were not alive with the limitless power of the great within. This inexhaustible brain capacity, however, can be developed by anyone, because the subconscious life of every cell is very easily awakened, and the more we draw upon this larger interior life, the easier it becomes to secure more The problem is to take the first step; that is, to enter into conscious touch with the subconscious side of things; and when this is done, we have the key that will unlock all the greater powers that are latent within us.

How to Proceed—To give more life and action to every part of the brain is necessary before real brain development can begin; but to promote this, the three great divisions of the brain must receive special and distinct attention. Each part must be dealt with according to its special function, and every effort to increase the life and action of that part must be animated with the desire to promote the power and efficiency of that function. The function of the fore brain embraces principally the power of intellect, memory and imagination. The mind acts directly upon this part of the brain when it reasons and knows, and also when it creates ideas, forms plans, evolves methods, analyzes laws and principles, understands, comprehends, discriminates, or exercises the elements of insight, perception or discernment. The function of the back brain embraces working capacity, force, determination, push, power, reserve force and kindred elements. The mind draws upon the back brain whenever force is required in the actual doing of things, and acts upon this part of the brain when trying to control, direct and master anything in the physical personality. The function of the top brain embraces aspiration, ambition, consciousness of quality and worth, attainments of superiority, perception of ideals and the realization of higher mental states of conscious existence. The mind acts through the top brain whenever it soars to greater heights, or whenever it builds for greater things anywhere in the physical or mental domain. When the top brain is large and active the finer things of life are readily discerned, but when this part of the brain is small or sluggish nothing is appreciated but that which can be weighed or measured.

Full Development—The combined use of all the different parts of the brain is necessary to secure results along any line. Every effort requires intelligence and imagination as well as power and working capacity. And no effort is worth while unless it is prompted by the desire to press on towards the greater, the superior and the ideal. Every part of the brain, therefore, should be well developed. Every part helps every other part, and the best results are secured along any line when all parts of the brain are equally developed. Abnormal development in some parts may give expression to exceptional genius, but such genius is one-sided. It is not properly balanced, and for that reason can never be at its best. When genius is queer, eccentric, peculiar, or addicted to what is called "the artistic temperament" it is not the best developed form of genius; it is not real genius, but the expression of extraordinary powers that are only under partial control; that is, they may be controlled to do great things through a certain faculty, but they are not controlled to act in harmony with all the faculties; and it is only when all the faculties act in harmony that the highest attainments and the greatest achievements become possible.

Real Genius—Where we find real genius we find exceptional capacity for work and remarkable talent for high efficiency. But we do not find such genius to be eccentric, very sensitive or difficult to get along with. The real genius is broad minded and can get along with anybody. He is a master mind and can therefore adapt himself to all kinds of conditions, and can use all kinds of conditions through which to reach the greater goal in view. The real genius is well balanced, and therefore has not simply the power to do great things, but also the power to live a great life. The reason why so many among those who possess certain grades of genius are eccentric or oversensitive, is found in the fact that certain parts of their brains are not sufficiently developed to act in harmony with those better developed parts through which the genius in question is expressed. But when these neglected parts become well developed, those people will not only become well balanced characters and charming personalities, but they will also gain the power to do greater things than ever before.

Building Brain Cells—To develop any part of the brain more energy and more nourishment will be required in that part, and these two essentials may be provided through subjective concentration. When we concentrate subjectively upon any part of the human system we produce more mental action in that part. This increase of mental action will cause more life and energy to be generated in that part. It will also attract surplus energy from other parts of the system because

much gathers more; and in brief, will increase
the circulation in that part, thus supplying the
added nourishment required.   When we concentrate upon any part of the brain we promote the
building of brain cells.   Wherever an increase of
energy and nourishment is provided the cell
building process will be promoted.   And if that
concentration is inspired with a strong desire
to attain the greater and the superior, the new
brain cells will have superior qualities.   Accordingly they will become fit instruments for the expression of real genius.   The concentration of
attention upon every part of the brain will also
cause all the inactive cells to become alive, though
in order to secure the best results in this respect
the mind should try to feel the finer forces of
the brain, and the finer activities of those forces
while concentration is taking place.   So long as
concentration is mechanical there are no results,
but when the process of concentration works
through the finer life forces it becomes a living
process, and the desired results will invariably
follow.

Special Methods—To build brain cells in any
part of the brain, and to cause all of the cells in
that part to become alive, concentration should
aim to promote the natural functions of that
part; that is, when we concentrate upon any part
of the brain we should express a strong, deep and

persistent desire to do that which that particular part has the natural power to do. When concentrating upon the back brain, be determined. Mentally act in the positive, determined attitude; desire power, and aim to push forward every purpose you have in view. Feel the increase of capacity and try to realize that the energies of the back brain are constantly accumulating, becoming stronger and stronger, until you feel as if you had sufficient power to see anything through. This process of concentration will accomplish three things. The inactive cells of the back brain will become alive. And the more living cells there are in any part of the human system the more power and capacity there will be in that particular part. Secondly, new brain cells will be formed; and as all of these new cells will be alive, there will be further increase in the power and the working capacity of the back brain. And third, the natural function of the back brain will be promoted. You will have more force and more push. You will become more positive and more determined, and your power to see things through to a finish will increase in proportion. In addition, there will be a steady increase of creative energy, and this is very important, because to possess an enormous amount of creative energy is one of the principal secrets of genius. When concentrating upon the fore brain use the imagination extensively. Create mental pictures of every mental state of being that you can imagine. Form plans of all kinds, and try to promote practical methods for every imaginable undertaking in the world. Use the power of analysis thoroughly upon every idea, law or principle that you may encounter in your thinking, and try to form your own original conclusion as to the nature of it all. Try to feel intelligence, and picture mental brilliancy in every cell throughout that part of the brain. But do not permit your thinking to become heavy or laborious. Keep attention in touch with the finer forces of the brain, and have expansion of mind constantly in view. This concentration will do for the fore brain what it was stated the previous exercise would do for the back brain, and in addition it will develop the power to create ideas of merit; and there is no mental power that is more important than this. Everything that man has formed in the visible world was first an idea. And as the best ideas produce the best results in practical life, we realize therefore, that those who develop the power to create better and better ideas will steadily rise in the scale, occupying more important places every year in the world's work. When concentrating upon the top brain aspire to the highest you know. Give full expression to all the powers of your ambition. Desire superiority, and try to feel consciously all the elements of worth that you know to have existence. Live in the ideal. Transcend the world of things and let your mind soar to empyrean heights. Think of everything that is high, noble and great, and desire with all the power of your soul to realize it all. Then know that you can. Have full confidence in yourself. Have faith in all your desires and ambitions. Think that you can. Feel that you can, and inspire that feeling with the loftiest thoughts that you can possibly form in your mind. Concentrate in this manner every day, or several times every day when convenient. A few minutes at a time is sufficient, and if done properly, a year's time will produce improvements that no one at first could believe.

Additional Methods—Another most excellent exercise is to concentrate upon every group of cells in the brain, giving a few seconds to each group, and then picture genius in every cell during the process. What we mentally picture, we create; therefore by daily picturing genius in every brain cell, we will tend to create genius in every brain cell. We thus develop the brain of the genius, and whatever we may wish to attain or accomplish we will then have a brain that can positively do what we wish to have done. To awaken and increase the subconscious life in the brain cells, the following method should be employed: Turn attention upon the back brain and think with deep feeling of the subconscious life that you know permeates every fibre. Continue for a few moments, and try to enter into this finer mental life. Do not be anxious for results, but be calm and well poised, and deeply determined to secure results. In a few moments move attention to the right of the brain and repeat the process. Then move attention to the left of the brain, repeating the process in each case. In each part try to enter into the finer subconscious life, and desire the awakening of this life with the deepest and strongest desire possible. The entire exercise may continue for ten or fifteen minutes, and may be taken once or twice a day.

Important—Pay no attention to the way you feel after the exercise. You may feel drowsy or you may feel mentally exhilarated. In either case keep calm, retain your poise and know that every brain cell in your possession has increased its volume of life and power. Immediately after the exercise relax mind and body. Let your thought pass down through the body so as to distribute equally among all the nerve centers the added life which you have gained. Then proceed to think of something else. The art of concentration, when fairly well mastered, may be exercised at any time. To use spare moments for this work is a most excellent practice, because it will not interfere with the regular duties, and besides it will make those mo-

FIG I.

1. Power.   2. Intellect   3. Aspiration

ments very interesting as well as highly valuable We may promote brain building at any time when engaged in work that is purely mechanical or that does not require direct attention; and in fact, we should try to train ourselves to build the brain at all times, no matter what our work may be. We should train the forces of the mind to pass through certain parts of the brain, so to speak, while doing their work, and we should expect those forces to promote development wherever they are directed to act. The energy employed in thinking should build brain cells and develop mental faculties during the process of thought, no matter what that thought might be. The same should be expected of energy employed in study or in any form of mental work, and all mental energy in action will promote brain and mind development when trained to do so.

CHAPTER II

MAKING EVERY BRAIN CELL ALIVE

The greater the number of active brain cells, the greater the supply of mental energy; and the more mental energy, the greater the power, the ability and the working capacity of the mind. Every active brain cell generates mental energy. To keep all the cells in action is to accumulate energy; and as much accumulates more, the practice of making alive all the brain cells every day will ere long give the mind far greater capacity and power. In the average brain only one half of the cells are active, and of those that are active only a fraction are thoroughly alive. That ability could be doubled and even trebled in the average mind through a practical system of brain development is therefore evident.

When a majority of the brain cells are dormant the mind is dull, stupid, and even lazy. When the cells in the back brain or in the lower part of the brain are dormant or partly so, a tendency to physical inactivity follows almost invariably. To remove this condition therefore, we must arouse the dormant cells in those parts

46

that are affected. The fact that a person is indolent or stupid does not indicate that there is nothing in him. In fact, he may have remarkable ability along certain lines, but not enough mental energy to put that ability into action. And a lack of mental energy is always due to inaction among the majority of the brain cells. Any person who is inclined to be sluggish in his activity can never do his best. He will accomplish only a fraction of what he has the latent power to accomplish, and will gain very little as far as comfort, happiness and attainment are concerned. An inactive person is never healthy, because there are too many dead cells in his system, and he cannot possibly enjoy life to any degree of satisfaction because his mind is partly in a stupor. His contentment, if he has any, will be the contentment of partial insensibility and not that which comes from having entered into harmony with the life that is alive. There is no real comfort in being sluggish or indolent. The man who takes it easy does not get one-third as much satisfaction from his life and his work as does the one who turns all his energy into his work, and who makes himself the very personification of industry, enterprise and achievement. The happiest man is the one who works with all his power and lives with all his life, but who works

and lives in poise. He is also the healthiest
man because a live personality is always wholesome and full of vitality.

When the entire personality is not thoroughly alive, waste matter will accumulate in various parts, clogging the blood vessels, obstruct-
ing the nerve forces and interfering in general
with the normal functions of the system. This
waste matter will also cause the tissues to
ossify, to harden, to wrinkle up and look old.
This is one reason why the man who retires
from business and tries to do nothing becomes
old very fast. A man, however, does not have
to remain in the business world all his life in
order to live a long and interesting life, but he
must keep his entire system alive and active.
And to do this, the first essential is to exercise
daily the cells of the brain and the cells of the
various nerve centers. The belief that no one
can afford to give time or attention to any other
part of the mind than that which is employed
directly in his vocation, is a mistake, because
when the whole of the mind is kept alive and
every brain cell is continued in action, the
amount of mental energy upon which any faculty may draw will increase to a very great
extent. True, those faculties that we use
directly in our leading occupations should be
developed to a greater degree than the rest of

the mind, but the whole of the mind and the whole of the brain should be put to work generating energy. The more energy any faculty may have at its command the greater its capacity for work, and the more thoroughly will its work be done. Every cell in the brain, therefore, should be employed in generating energy, so that the faculties we do employ may have unlimited power upon which to draw. The fact that an increase of mental energy will increase the ability and the working capacity of the mind, and the fact that strong minds, competent minds and able minds are in great demand everywhere makes this subject extremely important.

Another fact that must not be overlooked is that the brain is the instrument of the mind, and must, therefore, be placed in the best possible working condition before the mind can do justice to itself. If every other string in a piano were out of tune, no musician, not even the very best, could produce music through that instrument. But it is just as impossible for the mind to carry on real thinking with a brain wherein a large percentage of the cells are dormant. The fact that so few minds are able to think clearly or produce original thought on any desired subject is due almost entirely to the presence of so many inactive brain cells. Every dormant brain cell is an obstacle to mental action. The energies of thought cannot act upon or act through such cells. We therefore understand that the presence of such cells will interfere decidedly with the natural action of thinking, and that clear, consecutive, constructive thinking becomes almost impossible where dormant cells are numerous. The fact that the mind may be very active does not prove that all the brain cells are alive, because that activity may be confined almost entirely to certain limited portions of the brain; and the fact that most active brains tire easily proves that the majority of the cells are not doing anything. When all the brain cells are alive and generating energy, there will be so much energy in the brain that the mind will never feel tired, provided of course it works in poise; and the entire brain will naturally become transparent so that the mind can see through every thought, so to speak, and thus think clearly upon every subject. To emphasize this fact, we may add that every dormant cell is like a daub of paint upon a window pane, so therefore, we can realize how the presence of such cells will interfere with clear thought.

The belief that every part of brain and mind will be kept in action through an attempt to exercise all the mental faculties at frequent in-

tervals, is not true. First, because no one has
the time. To give five minutes of thought in
the field of every faculty would require from six
to eight hours, something that only a few could
do every day. And those few who might have
so much time on their hands would naturally
have neither the ambition nor the ability to
carry out such an extensive regime. Second,
to exercise thought in the field of a certain
faculty does not necessarily bring into action
all the brain cells in that particular part of the
brain where the said faculty functions. Ordinary thinking, about faculties, talents, qualities, attributes or definite subjects seldom
bring into play other cells than those already
in action. Nor does the direct use of the
faculty arouse all the cells in the field of action
in that faculty. The ordinary use of any part
of the mind simply draws upon the energy that
is already being generated without doing anything directly to arouse those cells that are
dormant. To stir up the dormant brain cells,
it will therefore be necessary to employ a different process; in fact, a special process, a
process, that will act upon every cell, and that
will have the power to arouse that cell into the
fullest possible action.

The process that we shall outline for this
work need not require more than ten minutes

of time each day, although it would be well to give the matter two or three times as much attention, and even that would be possible for anyone, no matter how busy he might be. It has been demonstrated conclusively that you can arouse to action any cells in the system by concentrating attention upon that cell, provided your mind is acting in a state of deep, but highly refined feeling at the time. To awaken a cell, however, it is not necessary to concentrate attention upon that one cell individually. Just as good results may be secured by concentrating upon a large group of cells; and this is especially true when attention aims to move in what may be termed the expansive attitude. To proceed, divide the brain into eight or ten parts, viewing each part as a special group of cells. Then concentrate subjectively for one, two or three minutes upon each group. Take this exercise every day and give it all the interest and enthusiasm that you can possibly arouse in your mind. In a few weeks every cell in your brain will be at work generating energy, and you will discover that the power and the working capacity of your mind will have almost doubled; but this will be only the beginning. If you continue this exercise, and try to make constructive use of all the added power you gain, you will soon come to the conclusion that your ability along any special line can be increased and developed to a remarkable degree. When concentrating in this manner upon each group of brain cells, try to picture mentally all the cells of that group that you can imagine as existing there. This will cause attention to penetrate the entire group through and through, and thus act upon each cell with the full force of thought. The fact that there are millions of cells in the brain need not disturb the imagination in its effort to mentally see them all. The imaging faculty is fully equal to the task. If not at first, it will become so after a little cultivation.

When concentrating upon the brain cells, there should be a strong, deeply felt desire to arouse every cell, but this desire should invariably act in perfect poise, and should never permit the slightest trace of forced action. To establish a full life, a wholesome life, a strong life, a wholly active life and a smooth, calm, harmonious life in every brain cell should be the purpose, and during the process of concentration the mind should be thoroughly determined to carry out this purpose. In many minds certain parts of the brain are very active, while other parts are not. Such minds, therefore, should give most of their attention and concentration to the inactive parts for a while, or until a balanced, thoroughly alive mental action is established in every part of the brain.

The process of concentration should begin at the lower part of the back brain, and should move forward gradually, ending at the upper part of the fore brain. During this concentration all the finer creative energies of the system should be drawn gently, with deep feeling and strong desire, towards the brain. And after the exercise is over, both mind and body should relax completely for a few moments, as this will produce perfect equilibrium. The result of this exercise, if taken daily, will be to eliminate all sluggishness, all stupidity, all dullness and all tendency to indolence or inactivity in any part of the mind, the brain or the nervous system. The mental power will increase remarkably, thinking will become clear and the brain will become such a perfect instrument that the mind can always do justice to itself no matter how highly it may be developed or how great its ambitions may be.

CHAPTER III

PRINCIPLES IN BRAIN BUILDING

The Leading Principle—To increase the size, to improve the quality and to multiply the energies of every faculty, talent or power that exists in the human mind, and to promote in general or in particular the development of ability, talent and genius, the leading principle is to combine the brain, the mind and the soul in every effort made to this end. This, however, is a new idea. No attempt has ever been made in the past to combine these three factors in an orderly and scientific manner for the promotion of any form of development; but we shall find as we proceed that it is this principle that constitutes the real secret of this important work. Many scientists have devoted themselves to the study of the brain. Many meta-physicians have searched for the mysteries of the mind. And others have spent a lifetime trying to fathom the depths of the soul, but no definite effort has been made to combine these three factors for practical results. But this we must do if we are to promote this system of development. And as we carry out this principle we shall find that there is no reason why anyone may not become as much and achieve as much as his loftiest ambitions hold in view. As this principle is applied the weakest mind can be made strong, the dullest mind can be made to improve constantly in activity and brilliancy, and such minds as are already brilliant can be improved to an extent that will in many instances approach the extraordinary.

The Process Simple—We shall understand presently how these exceptional possibilities can be realized. And we shall also find that the process involved is very simple. This, however, is natural, because the greatest things are always the simplest. This is one reason why we fail to find them at once, because there is a tendency in the human mind to look constantly for the complex, laboring under the delusion that the complex alone is great. But now we realize that man can improve himself only as he learns to get down to rock bottom and apply the laws of mental growth in their original simplicity. The obstacle that most of us have met is this, that instead of applying the laws of nature, we have tried instead to apply somebody's interpretation of those laws; but interpretations are usually complex, confusing and misleading, while the laws themselves are sufficiently simple for a child to comprehend and apply.

Important Questions—Proceeding directly to the consideration of this great subject, we will naturally find ourselves asking the following questions: What makes a mind great? Why does one person have ability and another not? What is talent and what does it come from? What is the secret of genius? What is the reason that some minds become so much and achieve so much while others accomplish practically nothing? These are important questions and there must be definite answers to them all; in fact, there must be an inner secret that makes the difference in each case. When we look at a person with a great mind we cannot at first find the secret, and as few are able to look beyond the exterior person, we have remained comparatively in ignorance on this great subject, admittedly one of the greatest of the ages. In most minds the secret of greatness, ability and genius is looked upon as a hidden something that can possibly not be found. But when we analyze man as he really is, and find that he is not simply personal, but mental and spiritual as well, this secret is no longer hidden. We find it to be composed of a few natural laws in orderly application. And we also find that both the understanding and the application of these laws are very simple.

Essentials Required—When we speak of ability in any particular mind, we usually consider only one or two faculties in that mind, as there are but few minds that are really great in more than two things. For this reason, to answer the questions presented above, we must analyze those individual faculties and try to discover why they are so remarkable. When we study such faculties, we find that there are three reasons why they are different from ordinary faculties; and these reasons are, that in all superior faculties we find size, quality and power exceptionally developed and properly combined. So this, therefore, is the simple secret of ability, talent and genius; and being so simple, we can readily understand why it has been overlooked. However, as we proceed in harmony with its natural simplicity, and try to apply it, we find that any one of these three essentials can be developed to almost any degree. And as the combined and harmonious application of the three essentials is a matter that anybody can master, we realize again that there is no reason why we all should not become much and achieve much. In fact, there need be no end to what we can develop and accomplish along any line. The talents we now possess can be developed far beyond anything we have ever imagined or dreamed of. And those greater powers that are still latent in the potential may be brought forth so that man will still accomplish what the race has never imagined possible.

Essentials Explained—Before we proceed further, it will be necessary to know what is really understood by the term size, quality, and power as applied to the faculties and talents of man; and also how those essentials were produced in such minds, as we have made no effort to develop and build through any method whatever. When we meet an exceptional mind we usually come to the conclusion that that mind secured remarkable ability and power without knowing anything about systems of development, and also that ability and genius are for this reason born in those who have them. To the average mind, this conclusion may seem to prove that only those can be able who are born able, and that therefore there can be no use for the ordinary mind in trying to develop added ability. But here we should remember that as it is possible to improve the trees and the flowers as well as all kinds of animals, there necessarily must be some way to improve man both physically, mentally and spiritually, as man needs improvement more than anything else, having greater responsibility, and being at the highest point, so to speak, of the creative powers of nature. We all must admit the logic of such ideas, but we need not depend upon logic. We also have the facts. We have the evidence in the case, and there is nothing more evident than evidence. The human mind as well as all the faculties and powers in man can be developed, and there is nothing to indicate that there is any end to the possibility of such development. We have found the secret, and that it works, is being demonstrated every day. The wise course to pursue, therefore, is to give our whole attention to the application of the laws and the methods involved, so that the best in view may be realized. The size of the faculty is determined by that part of the brain through which the faculty functions. The quality of the faculty comes from the state of the mind, and the power that enables the faculty to do its work comes from the within, and increases as the within is awakened and developed. To give a faculty size, therefore, we must deal with the brain. To give a faculty quality we must deal with the mind, and especially the states of the mind. And to give a faculty power we must deal with the soul, or rather the entire interior realms of life and consciousness. Thus we understand why the brain, the mind and the soul must be combined if we wish to provide the three essentials—size, quality, and power—required in the increase of ability or genius along any line.

Further Explanation—The reason why these three essentials are required can be simply illustrated. The engine must have steam or it will not have the power to do what it is built to do. It may be very large and have enormous capacity, but if there is little or no steam it can do practically nothing. Then the engine may have any amount of steam to draw upon, but if it is very small it cannot use all of this power, and will accordingly accomplish but little. Then again the engine may be large and the steam abundant, but if it is poorly constructed it will not work. In other words, if the engine is to perform its purpose, it must have size, quality and power, and the more it has of these three, the more it can do. It is exactly the same with the human mind, and when we realize this we understand why so many large brains accomplish nothing, why so many fine minds accomplish nothing, and why so many strong minds accomplish nothing. The large brain must have mental quality back of it, and abundance of creative energy from the subconscious. The fine mind must have plenty of power back of it, and a large brain through

which to act.   The strong soul must have
mental quality so as to give its power superior
ideas with which to work, and a large brain
through which these superior ideas can find
full expression.

Increase of Size—It is therefore evident that
those who wish to become much and accomplish something of worth must give their attention to the three essentials mentioned, and to
give special attention to that essential that is
most deficient in development.   If you have a
large well developed brain, but low mental
quality with but little power, give your attention principally to the development of mind
and soul.   But if you have plenty of energy
and ambition with good mental quality, but a
poorly developed brain, give your attention to
the brain, and have its size increased especially
in those parts through which the talent you
desire naturally functions.   And here we must
remember that each faculty functions through
a special part of the brain—a fact that is not
only important, but that is in perfect harmony
with the laws of nature.   The function of sight
employs the eye while that of hearing employs
the ear.   The other senses have their own particular channels, and the same is true of the
various faculties of the mind.   Each individual
faculty finds expression through its own part

of the brain, and therefore it is necessary that that particular part be well developed if the faculty in question is to function with exceptional ability and power. The increase of size, therefore, in any part of the brain becomes a matter that will require the very best attention we can possibly provide, though the process through which this increase may be brought about is very simply applied. It is a well known fact that any part of the system will grow and develop in size if more nourishment and vitality is supplied; and increased nourishment and vitality can readily be supplied by increasing the circulation in that particular part. This is a fact that has been thoroughly demonstrated, so that we may proceed with the full conviction that as we apply the principle involved we shall positively secure the desired result.

Interesting Experiments—The following experiments will illustrate how nourishment and vitality can be increased in any part of the physical form: Place a dog's paw in a vacuum at stated intervals for some period of time, and that paw will become twice as large as the other one. And the explanation is that the vacuum draws more blood into the paw thus providing additional nourishment and vitality. The same experiment can be applied along a number of other lines, proving the same idea; but here we may enquire how increased circulation can be produced in any part of the brain. We can not employ mechanical means for such a purpose; therefore, must find another plan. It is admitted that added development will naturally take place wherever there is an increase of nourishment and vitality; and this increase is supplied by an increase of the circulation in that part; but the problem is, how to increase the circulation in any part of the brain. The solution, however, is simple, as the following experiments will illustrate: Place a man upon an oscillating platform, and have him so placed that the body is perfectly balanced, the feet and the head being at equal distance from the floor; then tell him to work out a difficult problem, or tell him to think of something that requires very deep thought. In a few seconds the circulation will increase in the brain sufficiently to cause the head to go down considerable, and even to the floor, as the feet or the other end of the body rises accordingly. Here is an illustration of how the circulation can be increased in the brain simply by carrying out a certain line of thought. Then tell this same man to imagine that he is running a foot race, and in a few seconds the circulation will increase in the feet to such an extent that the feet will become heavier than the head, and go down as the head goes up. This is an experiment that most anyone can try with most interesting results, and it gives tangible evidence to prove that the mind can control the circulation. While the mind was thinking about the deep problem, extra energy and circulation was drawn to the brain; but when that same mind was imagining the running of a foot race, this extra energy and circulation went towards the feet because attention was concentrated upon the feet at the time. Another interesting experiment is to imagine yourself taking a hot foot bath. You will soon find your feet becoming very warm, the veins beginning to swell, indicating that increased circulation has been produced in that part of the body. Here we have the same principle; that is, the power of mind to increase the circulation in any part of the body by concentrating with deep interest upon that particular part. A number of similar experiments can be carried out, proving the same law; and as the law is so simply applied, we find that there is no reason whatever why the increase of the size of any part of the brain may not be produced as we may desire.

Power of Concentration—To apply this law we must understand how to concentrate. If we concentrate simply in an objective sense, we have no effect upon the forces of the system, and the above law will not act. But when we concentrate subjectively, that is, with deep interest and feeling, we find that the forces of the system invariably accumulate at the point of concentration; and where the forces of the system accumulate, an increase in circulation will invariably follow. To explain this matter more fully, we might state that real concentration upon any part of the body causes mind and consciousness to increase activity in that part. Wherever there is an increase of mental activity, the finer life currents will become more active; and where those currents become more active the circulation will increase. This is how the law operates, and it is based entirely upon how deeply the mind feels at the time of concentration, and how deeply interested the attention is in the project we wish to carry out. In other words, it is the concentration that is felt that controls the circulation, because such concentration acts through the finer forces of the system; and the circulation is controlled by those finer forces.

Deep Feeling Necessary—The above may seem to lead us into difficulties, and take away the ease and simplicity that was previously indicated; but we need not be disturbed. This inner consciousness of finer feeling is simply secured, and what is better still, we all have it already. What we wish to make perfectly clear is the fact that you cannot draw additional vitality and nourishment to any part of the brain unless you concentrate your attention upon that part while your mind feels the action of the finer life current. You do not govern functions or activities anywhere in your system until you act through subjective mentality because all physical functions, including the circulation, are controlled by the subconscious mind. Whenever you feel deeply, however, you act directly upon the subconscious, and may, therefore, originate and direct any new subconscious act desired. The principle is to feel deeply whenever you concentrate. Nothing else need be attempted. If you know that you feel deeply whenever you turn your attention to any part of the brain, you will know that there will be an increase of nourishment and vitality in that part, and that the brain cells of that part will be developed and built up accordingly.

Unconscious Development—In answering the question why a great many minds have been developed without the understanding of this law, we need simply state that it is possible to use some of the most important laws of mind and body without really understanding the nature of those laws. In fact, we are doing this all the time. When you wish to succeed in any undertaking, and you concentrate all your efforts upon that purpose, you develop to a certain extent the faculty employed in that undertaking. And the reason is that the concentration that was unconsciously practiced caused the added nourishment and vitality to be supplied to that part of the brain through which the faculty in question was expressed. In other words, you employ unconsciously the same law that we are trying to use consciously and according to exact science. But here we must remember that although the unconscious use of a certain law may produce results, the conscious and intelligent use of that same law will naturally produce far greater results. Therefore, we wish to understand the inside secret of this entire theme, so that we can make the best use of all the principles involved.

The Power of Ambition—In this same connection we learn that ambition is also a channel through which unconscious development is constantly taking place. When you have a strong ambition to realize a certain goal, the force of that ambition naturally tends to build up those faculties that you need in order to reach your goal. And we find that the force of ambition also involves the force of concentration, because we always concentrate upon those things that we are deeply ambitious to realize. We find, therefore, that both the mind and the brain may be built up through the exercise of a strong, determined ambition. But here as elsewhere, we should not be satisfied simply with the unconscious use of the principle involved. If we would, instead of simply being ambitious, proceed to direct the force of ambition upon that part of the brain through which the desired talent naturally functions, we would find that that talent would develop with far greater rapidity than through the old general method of simply being ambitious; in other words, we would have another illustration of the power of concentration and intelligent action.

Illustration—To illustrate this idea further, we will suppose that you are ambitious to become a great musician, but instead of being simply ambitious, you concentrate you mind upon that part of the brain through which the faculty of music functions. The result will be that the power of your ambition will express itself directly in building up your musical faculty, because the additional mental energy that you will provide for that faculty will not only build up the mind in that part, but will also tend to supply additional nourishment and vitality for the corresponding part of the brain. Here we find a new use for that great mental force usually called ambition, especially since it can be employed in the building up of any faculty whatever. We realize that those who will make the right use of this force in building up any faculty, the increased development of which is desired, will naturally secure decided results from the very beginning; and if the process is continued with perseverance, will secure results that will be nothing less than remarkable. In this part of our study we have given special attention to size as previously defined, and have illustrated how size could be secured by building up any part of the brain. Later on, we shall consider quality and power. But we should all remember in pursuing this study that size is of exceptional importance, the fact being that there are very few brains that are sufficiently developed to give the proper expression to the ability and the genius that most of us already possess.

CHAPTER IV

PRACTICAL METHODS IN BRAIN BUILDING

Important Faculty—The power of the mind is limitless; that is, the power that is already active in the mind can, as it is directed, reproduce itself in larger and larger quantities. This faculty is latent in every mind, and is employed to some degree by every mind. The more mental power we generate, the greater becomes the mental capacity to generate more. But only as much of the power of the mind can be expressed as the development of the brain will permit. Therefore, the cultivation of the mind and the increase of mental power will not produce an increase in ability, talent and genius unless the brain is developed just as thoroughly as the mind.

The Highly Organized Brain—To develop the brain there are three essentials that must be constantly promoted. First, every brain cell must be made more active; second, the number of brain cells must be increased; and third, the brain as a whole must be more highly organized. Dormant brain cells obstruct the expression of ability and power, while active brain cells tend to promote that expression. An active brain cell not only permits the expression of mental power, but actually calls forth more and more of that power. The more brain cells you have, the more channels for mental expression you will have, and the greater the number of these channels, the greater your mental capacity. The highly organized brain is superior in quality, and, therefore, can respond readily to the highest forms of genius. The brain that is gross, crude or dense cannot act as an instrument for any form of genius, not even for the simplest forms of practical ability; and the fact that most brains are crude and undeveloped, either as a whole or in parts, explains why extraordinary ability is the exception rather than the rule.

Ability Trebled—Extraordinary ability need not remain the exception, however; there are thousands of minds with ordinary ability that would double and treble their ability by simply taking a thorough course of brain development. They already have the mental power, but their brains are not sufficiently developed to give full expression to that power. And there are other thousands who are not conscious of any talents whatever that would become talented if their brains were sufficiently developed to give full expression to all that is in them. A thorough development of the brain will also reveal what a person is best adapted for, for when every faculty can fully express itself, it is an easy matter to discover which one is the strongest; and if that one is given further development, extraordinary ability will be the result.

More Brain Cells—To know how much you can do through any faculty, is not possible until every cell in the brain is fully alive, and when you do discover what you can do through any special faculty, you can double your ability in that faculty by doubling the subconscious power back of that faculty, and by doubling the number of cells in that part of the brain through which that faculty functions. To double the number of cells in the brain, or in any part of the brain, is possible without increasing the usual size of the cranium, because the cells invariably decrease in size as the structure of the brain is improved in quality. The smaller the cells of the brain the better; and the more active and the more highly organized the brain, the more nearly the brain cell approaches the form of a mere point of expression. And for the same reason, the smaller the cells of the brain, the more easily and the more thoroughly can the mind concentrate upon any special subject.

The Vital Secret—To make every cell alive, the secret is to concentrate attention upon every part of the brain, thinking of the finer substance of the brain at the time, and proceeding with the desire to promote increase in life, energy and power. Turn attention first upon the center (a point midway between the opening of the ears) and think of the finer life and substance that permeates the region of that center. Then, while in that deeper state of thought and feeling, move attention through any part of the brain you like, and toward the surface. This movement should be gradual, and you should try to deeply feel and gently arouse the finer life that permeates the brain cells through which your thought is passing. When your concentration comes to the surface of the brain, move it back again gradually, passing through the same region until you come to the brain center. Take about two minutes for the process of passing concentration from the brain center to any part of the surface of the brain and back again to the center. This exercise may last from ten to twenty minutes and should be taken once a day, but should never be taken immediately after a meal.

Subjective Concentration—When you concentrate upon any part of the brain, do not think of the physical brain, or the physical brain cells, but think of that finer or metaphysical substance that permeates the physical cells. This will hold concentration in the subjective state; and all concentration must be subjective to be effective. All actions of concentration should move smoothly, easily, deeply, and harmoniously; the process should be animated with a deep, calm, self-possessed enthusiasm; be positively, but calmly determined to secure results, and constantly expect results. Think of the brain as a perfect instrument of genius, and hold such a mental picture of the brain in your thought at all times.

The Real Principle—The number of cells in any part of the brain may be increased by concentrating subjectively upon that part. Whenever you concentrate attention upon any group of cells, you cause creative energy to accumulate in that group. Wherever creative energy accumulates, the circulation will increase, and in consequence there will not only be an increase of the power that builds, but also added nourishment with which to build. This is the principle: Concentrate upon any part of the brain, and you bring more energy and more nourishment to that part; and when more energy and more nourishment meet in any place, there will be more cells in that place. Concentration will cause these two essentials to meet wherever you may desire. But the concentration must be subjective; that is, do not concentrate upon the physical part of the brain, but upon that finer life and substance that permeates the physical. If you do not realize the existence of those finer life forces that permeate the physical cells, imagine the existence of finer cells as being within the physical cells, and concentrate upon those finer cells. You will soon begin to realize the finer substance and the finer life that fills or permeates the physical cells, and in the meantime you will have results; you will build the brain; you will develop those parts of the brain wherein you concentrate subjectively and with regularity.

Where to Concentrate—To impress ability in any faculty, concentrate regularly upon any part of the brain through which the faculty in question functions. Every leading faculty employs its own part, or parts, of the brain. Some faculties express themselves through one part only, while other faculties employ several parts. When you know what part of the brain is employed by some special faculty, build up that part; that is, concentrate daily upon that part and aim, not only to increase the number of cells, but also to refine and develop those cells. You will thus give your special faculty a more perfect instrument with which to work, and that faculty will steadily become stronger, more able and more efficient.

Improved Quality—The predominating thought of the mind during any period of concentration will determine the quality of the new cells that are conceived during that period. Therefore, to improve the quality of the brain cells and make

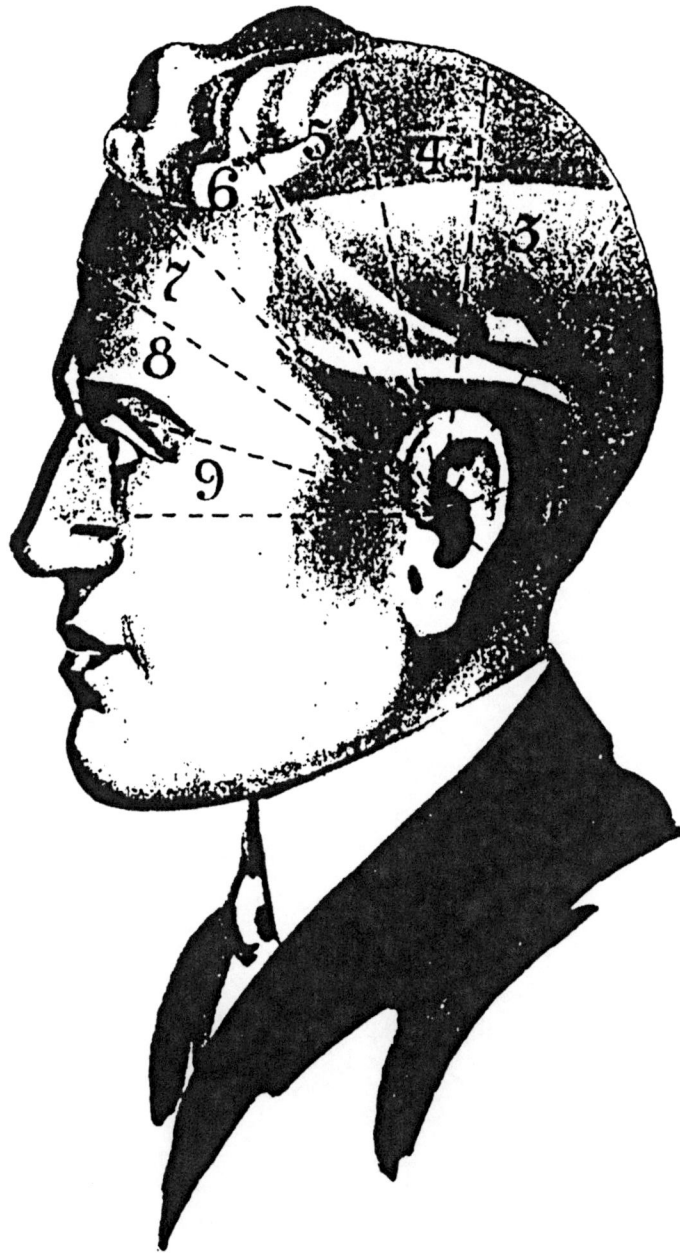

FIG. III.

1. Creative Energy
2. Love
3. Individuality
4. Interior
   Understanding
5. Emotion
6. Intuition
7. Intelligence
8. Application
9. Expression

the brain structure more highly organized, the quality of thought that is formed in mind during any exercise in concentration should be the highest that can possibly be imagined. When you concentrate upon any part of the brain, think of quality, refinement, worth, superiority, power, ability, talent, genius. Think of all these things in their highest forms and draw upon your imagination for higher and higher forms. Enrich your thinking to the very highest degree possible; this richer, higher, superior thought will permeate the very life and essence of every cell in your brain, and thus you will constantly improve this quality of your entire brain. When you concentrate upon any special part of your brain, use the same method, and in addition, picture in mind the superior genius of that faculty that functions through this special part. Try to impress this picture of superior genius upon every cell in that part of the brain, and try to feel that the spirit of superior genius is alive in every cell. You thus develop both the faculty and that part of the brain through which the faculty functions.

All Around Development—The balanced brain should be the first object in view. No matter what your vocation may be, every part of your brain should be well developed. The balanced brain has always the greatest capacity and the greatest endurance, because those parts that are not employed directly furnish added power to those parts that are employed directly. The balanced brain is also the most practical, having the power both to create ideas and the power to make actual use of those ideas. Compare the shape of your own brain with that of Figure II and you will see at once where the greatest amount of development is required in your own case. But do not give your whole attention to those parts that seem to be small; proceed to develop your whole brain so as to make every cell alive, and aim to improve the quality of your entire brain; give most of your time, however, to those parts that lack in size and activity. If your brain seems to be fairly well balanced, give most of your time to those parts that you employ directly in your daily work and the remainder of your time to the entire brain in general.

Where to Begin—Begin your development of the brain by taking from ten to twenty minutes every day and concentrate for a minute or two on the nine fundamental divisions outlined in Fig. III. Always begin with the region of "creative energy," and close with the region of expression. To increase creative energy is always the first essential in every undertaking; and expression is the final outcome, the climax, the goal in view. When you concentrate upon the region of creative energy, think deeply of accumulation, and try to feel the possession of limitless power. Be in perfect poise and harmony, and realize that your back brain is actually becoming charged with tremendous energy. Be as quiet as possible, try to hold it all in your system, and feel deeply so that the process of concentration will be subjective. When concentration ceases to be subjective, you lose your hold upon energies, and development will be interrupted; but so long as your concentration continues to be subjective, you will hold your energy in your system, you will also awaken more, and every desire for development will promote development.

Individuality—The largest conception of love that you can possibly realize should be deeply felt when you concentrate upon the region of "love." Think of everything that is tender, lovable and sweet; in fact, enter into the very world of immeasurable love; try to feel that you are absolutely at one with everything that is, and that you love with all your heart everything that is. The region of "individuality" is the principal channel of expression for the will; therefore when you concentrate upon the brain cells in this region, proceed to will with all the power of will. This region is also the principal seat of stability, firmness, self-confidence and faith. Accordingly, your desire to express these qualities should be combined with your own concentration. When you concentrate for the development of individuality enter into the spirit of faith; have faith in yourself; have faith in everybody and everything; have faith in your mission in life; have faith in the Supreme and have faith in faith. Be strong and firm; feel through and through that you are yourself—your superior self, and that you can master everything that is in yourself.

Discerning the Within—The inner world of things, as well as the higher side of things, is discerned through "interior understanding." It is also the channel through which the mind acts when we try to discern the ideal, the superior and those elements of true worth that exist within all things, and in the higher life of all things. When you concentrate upon this part of the brain think of the ideal, the higher, the greater, the superior, and try to mentally enter into the soul of your every thought. As you develop interior understanding you will gain the power to understand the metaphysical nature as well as the physical nature of all life, and no one can fully understand life, properly use life, or master life, until he can look at all things both from the metaphysical and the physical points of view.

Feeling the Real—When concentrating upon the region of "emotion" every effort should be made to enter into the most tender feelings of the soul; but all tendencies towards the sentimental should be avoided. Try to feel sympathetic; try to sympathize most keenly with everything and everybody, and try to realize the sublime state of oneness with the higher side of all that is. When trying to develop sympathy do not think of that which is wrong, pitiful or distressing; this will simply develop morbidity, a condition that is frequently mistaken for real sympathy. The true function of sympathy is to place the mind in touch with the real, the true, the sublime and the beautiful; in brief, to feel the touch of life; not false life, imperfect life, or misdirected life, but the life that is life, the life that makes all life truly worth while. The more perfectly we develop the finer emotions, the more keenly we can enjoy that something that may well be termed the music of sublime existence, and the more readily can we rise to those lofty heights in consciousness where we can see all things from all points of view. Therefore when we concentrate upon the region of emotion, we should try to enter into the music of sublime existence; we should try to rise to the mountain tops of consciousness; we should try to feel the tender touch of everything that is real, beautiful and true, and we should try to realize that something within us that binds the soul of man to every breathing, living thing in all the vastness of the cosmos.

Function of Intuition—Interior insight, discernment, judgment, decisions and all the finer perceptions of the mind function through that part of the brain termed "intuition." Intuition is indispensable, no matter what our vocation may be, because we are constantly called upon to decide as to what step to take further, or to judge as to the best course to pursue, or to look through this matter or that. It is a faculty, however, that has never been developed, and that is the principal reason why practical minds make so many mistakes, adopt the wrong plans almost at every turn, and so frequently walk right into failure when they could just as easily walk directly into success. The most successful men in the world possess natural intuition to a very great degree, and that is why they usually do the right thing at the right time. They know real opportunities when they see them, and they know when and how to take advantage of those opportunities. But they do not know these things through external evidence; they usually go contrary to external evidence and what is called safe and sane business sense. They follow a "finer business sense." They may not call their superior business judgment intuition, but it is the same thing, and it may be developed to a remarkable degree by

anyone. Proceed first to make alive and build up
that part of the brain through which this faculty
functions. Concentrate for a few minutes upon
this region several times a day, and especially
just before you are to decide upon some important
matter. While concentrating, think of interior
insight, try to see through every thought or idea
that enters the mind at the time, and desire deeply
to see the real truth in everything of which you
are conscious. Learn to depend upon your interior insight at all times, whenever you are
called upon to judge, select, look through or decide; and the constant use of this faculty in practical life, combined with daily concentration upon
this part of the brain, will develop this faculty to
almost any degree desired.

Building Intellect—Mental brilliancy and rare
mental activity may be developed by concentrating
upon the region of "intelligence." Think of pure
intellect and picture in mind the highest form of
mental brilliancy imaginable when concentrating
upon this part of the brain. Also, enter the feeling of mental expansion and limitless intellectual
capacity, and try to picture calmness and lucidity
in every thought you think. You thus, not only
develop and enlarge that part of the brain through
which pure intellect functions, but you also become more brilliant; and at the same time your
power to think, understand, comprehend and

realize is steadily increased. This method, if practiced for a few minutes several times a day, will, in the course of a few years, produce a prodigious intellect. There is no reason, therefore, why anyone should remain in a state of mental inferiority. Rare mental brilliancy and remarkable intellectual capacity are possible to all, but the high places are for those only who will go to work and make their possibilities come true.

Producing Results—Practical application is the art of combining the world of ideas with the world of things; or, rather, the turning of ideas into actual use. The faculty of "intelligence" produces the idea; the faculty of application puts that idea to work. To develop the faculty of application, concentrate upon that part of the brain marked "8" in Fig. II, and think of system, method and scientific application at the time. Impress upon every cell in that part of the brain a deep, positive desire to do things, and you will develop the "knack" of being practical, as well as increase the actual power of application.

The Real Purpose—The great climax of all life, all thought, all effort, is expression. The real purpose of man is to bring forth all that is in him—the whole of himself, and although every force and element in his system is employed, directly or indirectly, in promoting expression, the entire process is governed by the mind acting through a certain part of the brain. This part is the region marked "9" in Fig. II, and therefore as this region is more fully developed, the power to promote expression will increase in proportion. Some faculties employ this part of the brain directly, while all the other faculties employ it indirectly. The singer, the orator, the actor, the artist, the writer and the man who sells things, employ the faculty of expression directly; therefore, all such people should develop this part of the brain to the highest possible degree. But all others should give the faculty of expression thorough attention, because we all must express ourselves if we would be much and do much. When concentrating upon this part of the brain, think of the perfect expression of that which you desire to express more fully. If you are an artist, mentally see the expression of the ideal and the beautiful. If you are a singer, mentally feel the expression of tone. If you are an orator, mentally feel the power of eloquence. If you are a writer, mentally realize the expression, in language, of the ideas that you wish to express in literature. If you talk much, or write much, in a business way, with a view of promoting the sale of your product, mentally see yourself expressing yourself in the most forceful, the most persuasive and the most effective manner imaginable. Imagine yourself expressing yourself as you wish to express yourself, whenever you concentrate upon this part of the brain; and do not fail to draw upon your imagination for the most perfect expression possible. Impress upon your brain cells the greatest thoughts that you can imagine, and you thus train your brain to become a perfect instrument for the expression of those thoughts. In the general development of expression, desire deeply to express the best that is in yourself whenever you concentrate, and try to feel the all that is in yourself coming forth in an ever increasing measure.

Special Rules—It is important to remember that all concentration for brain development should begin at the brain center. First, turn attention upon the brain center; gently draw, with your thought, all the finer forces of the mind towards this center; then move the action of concentration toward the surface of the brain, thus passing through that region that you wish to develop. Move the action of concentration to and fro from the center of the brain to the surface, but give more attention to those groups of cells that lie near the surface of the brain, as it is these through which the mind functions to the greatest degree.

What to Expect—The time required to secure results through these methods will depend upon present development and how faithfully this process of development is applied. Results will usually begin to appear in a few days, and very marked results within a few weeks. An increase of mental life, mental power and mental capacity will be noted almost from the very beginning, and a decided improvement in practical efficiency will shortly follow. After a few weeks or a few months, you will discover that your general ability is growing, and at times, you will feel the power of genius finding expression through one or more of your faculties. You will then begin to realize that it is only a matter of perseverance in the daily application of these methods, when ability, talent and genius of the highest order will be attained.

When to Exercise—Apply these methods at any time or anywhere whenever you have a few moments to spare. Take twenty minutes once or twice a day, for regular practice if you can; and it is an excellent practice to use spare moments, as they come, for this purpose. Make it a point to concentrate for development upon some part of your brain whenever you have a minute or two. And, if you concentrate properly, you will not only reinvigorate the brain, but you will rest the mind from its regular work. Proper concentration is always subjective; that is, in the field of deeper, finer feeling. Never begin to concentrate until you feel deeply serene, and feel that your mind is acting calmly in those finer elements and forces that permeate the physical cells. To enter this subjective or finer state of thought and feeling, become very quiet for a few moments; breathe deeply but gently, and do not move a muscle; when you inhale, imagine that you are drawing the force of your personality into that finer subconscious life that permeates your personality; and when you exhale, imagine that all the forces of your system are moving down through your personality toward your feet. What you imagine you do during this exercise, you very soon will do; then you can master your forces in any way desired by simply thinking of your forces as doing what you wish them to do. During these breathing exercises, turn your attention upon the inner life of your system; try to feel this life, and try to enter mentally into the vast interior world of this life. You will soon realize that there is another world of force within the physical world of force. You are then in the subjective state; you are then in touch with the real power within you— the power that lies beneath every cell, and that can therefore change, reproduce or develop every cell. You may then proceed with your concentration; and this deeper power with which you are in touch will proceed to do whatever your predominant thought may desire at the time.

CHAPTER V

VITAL SECRETS IN BRAIN BUILDING

Remarkable Possibility—The brain is the instrument of the mind or the channel through which the unbounded possibilities of the mind are to find expression. It is therefore of the highest importance that the brain receive the most thorough and the most perfect development possible. The reason for this is readily understood when we learn that the average mind could do two or three times as much if the brain was properly developed, and that the quality of the work done could be improved not less than ten fold in many instances. It is a well known fact that the better the instrument, the better the results, other things being equal, and that no performer can do justice to himself unless his instrument is perfect. But this fact has not been considered in connection with the mind and its instrument. In consequence thereof not one person in ten thousand is giving his mind a fair chance.

Special Exercises Required—That the brain needs development, is admitted by everybody, but there is a current belief that the brain naturally develops as the mind develops, and that to exercise the brain in the mere act of thinking is sufficient to promote this development. This conclusion is based upon the idea that the mind is the unconscious builder of the brain, and that therefore the brain will be at each stage of mental development exactly what the mind requires it to be. But it would be difficult to find a more serious mistake than this. That the mind is the builder of the brain is true in a sense; that is, every change in the brain will be determined by the actions of the mind, and it is the mind that governs the chemical and creative processes that carry on construction and reconstruction. But that function of the mind that governs construction is a distinct function, and is not directly connected with the process of thinking. Thinking in itself does not necessarily develop the brain, nor does ordinary work always develop the muscles of the body. If thinking developed brains and working developed muscle, we should all be marvels of mental capacity and physical power. But the fact that the average person remains undeveloped both in mind and body, no matter how much he thinks or works, proves that special exercises are required for every form of development.

Two Distinctive Processes—To bring a crude, sluggish and perverse brain up to the highest state of action by mere thinking, is just as impossible as it is to bring a discordant piano into perfect tune by mere playing. To play the piano is one thing. To tune a piano or build a more perfect piano is quite another thing. In like manner, the regular creation or thinking of thought and the reconstruction of a more perfect physical brain are two distinct processes, and accordingly require different applications of the mind. It is man who builds the musical instrument, and it is man who employs that instrument to produce music. According to the same analogy, it is the mind that determines what its physical instruments are to be, and it is the mind that acts upon those instruments when thought or expression are to be produced. It is the mind, therefore, that must develop the brain. But the application of the mind in brain development is far different than that of usual thinking.

How Exercise Develops—To apply the mind in brain development, we must eliminate the belief that the use of anything in mind or body necessarily promotes the development of the thing used. It is not use or exercise in itself that develops. It is the extra supply of nourishment and energy that is drawn to the place through use or exercise that alone can promote development. The process of construction in body or brain is not possible without nourishment and creative energy. Therefore, when we increase the supply of these two in any part of the system we cause that part to develop more rapidly. The exercise of the muscle or faculty, however, does not always draw more nourishment and energy to those places where the exercise occurs. If it did, we should have physical giants and mental giants by the millions. And what is important, it is not the exercise itself that draws the circulation or the increased energy to those parts that are being exercised; it is the attitude of the mind that we sometimes enter while body or brain is in action. This is a discovery of exceptional value because when once understood all systems of mental or physical culture will be revolutionized. Instead of systems that produce occasional and accidental results, we shall then have systems that produce definite and positive results in every case. In brief, the idea is that physical or mental exercise does not draw increased circulation and increased energy to the part exercised unless the mind is in a certain attitude at the time; and it is absolutely necessary that increased circulation and increased energy be supplied at the point of exercise if development is to take place.

Subjective Concentration—That attitude of mind that invariably draws nourishment and energy to the part that is exercised is called subjective concentration, and the fact that it is subjective concentration and not exercise, in itself that develops, is a fact that all should understand more perfectly who have greater development for mind or body in view. Whenever any muscle is used, the act attracts attention and the mind will naturally concentrate upon that muscle to a degree. If the concentration is subjective, more nourishment and energy will be drawn to that muscle with development as the result. But if the concentration is not subjective, no added supply of nourishment or energy will be provided. The result will be that the muscle that is being exercised or used will use up the nourishment and energy already there and finally become tired or exhausted. No development, therefore, of that muscle can under the circumstances take place.

Accidental Development—In this connection we may well ask how people have succeeded in developing muscles and faculties before subjective concentration was understood. We know that a large number who have been ignorant of this mode of concentration have improved themselves through various systems. Then how did they do it? The secret is this; whenever you concentrate attention in the attitude of whole-hearted interest, you enter the subjective to a degree and thus concentrate subjectively without being aware of the fact. No matter what system of culture you employ, if you are not interested in the exercise you gain absolutely nothing; but on the other hand, the most perfect system will help you if you are thoroughly interested in the exercise. And the reason is that when you are interested you concentrate subjectively to a degree, and it is through that subjective concentration that you get your results. This idea is well illustrated by the fact that we are always helped the most by those methods that arouse our deepest interest and our most wide-awake attention. By being interested in our work, our studies and our exercises, we have accidentally, so to speak, entered to a degree into subjective moods of concentration, and through such concentration have drawn much nourishment and energy to the parts exercised, thus promoting development in a measure. To depend upon accidental or occasional results, however, will not and should not satisfy those who have greater things in view. We have scientific, exact and unfailing methods for reaching every goal and brain development is no exception. Therefore, we should find the best methods and apply them thoroughly so that every effort we make towards improvements will positively produce results.

Deep Interest—Since more nourishment and more energy are required where development is to take place, and since these two essentials will be provided wherever we concentrate in the subjective attitude, we understand why subjective concentration is the real secret to brain development as well as all other forms of development. For this reason we should enter the subjective attitude directly before we begin to concentrate, and not depend upon indirect means to produce this necessary attitude. By entering directly into the subjective attitude before we begin our concentration we shall have positive results in every instance, and thus avoid unnecessary delays. But if you feel that you do not clearly understand the idea of the subjective, use the term "deep interest" instead. The two terms mean the same. That is, become deeply interested in that upon which you proceed to concentrate, and train yourself to think, study and work in an attitude of deep feeling. Thus you will concentrate subjectively in the most natural and the most perfect manner, and invariably accomplish what you have in view.

Living Brain Cells—The discovery that the development of brain and body can be promoted thoroughly and rapidly through subjective concentration will prove valuable beyond belief because every brain almost is in such great need of special development. That a fine mind can work properly through a brain that is crude or sluggish is impossible, and yet the majority of brains are very crude in places and so sluggish in parts that hardly any activity is evident. It is a matter of fact that many parts of the average brain are almost entirely dormant—a condition that no one should permit to continue for a moment, because the full capacity of mind can find expression only when every cell in the brain is thoroughly alive. To bring life and full action into every cell, and to cause every cell to continue to be a living cell, attention should be concentrated subjectively upon every part of the brain several times each day. Ten minutes three times a day will produce great improvements within a few months. Then let no one say that he has not the time. The truth is we have not the time to neglect this matter. The possibilities that are within us are marvelous to say the least, but those possibilities cannot express themselves through a brain that is crude, sluggish or undeveloped.

Finer States of Action—To refine the substance of the brain is highly important, because it is only through a refined brain that superior mental qualities can find expression. For this reason a refining process should permeate the entire brain several times every day, or it may be applied in conjunction with regular concentration for development. While concentrating upon the brain, try to perceive or feel the finer elements of the brain that permeate the physical elements. This will draw the entire developing process into a finer state of action, which will tend to refine more and more every cell in the entire brain structure. To comprehend the finer elements of life and to gain conscious power of that something that is within things, beneath things, and above things, is absolutely necessary if we desire to become as much as nature has given us the power to become. But to respond to the life of that finer something, the brain must be so highly developed or refined in its substance and essence that every trace of crudeness and materiality has been removed. A clear understanding of all the finer processes of life and action will aid remarkably in giving this refinement and responsiveness to the brain, because every ascending tendency of the mind will, if applied to the brain, give higher and finer states of action to all the elements and forces of the brain.

Additional Results—When subjective concentration is perfectly understood and thoroughly applied, we shall find that in addition to continuous development of the brain, all undesirable conditions will be removed from the mind. No forms of mental exhaustion, lack of mental energy or mental depression of any kind will ever occur so long as the brain is properly supplied with nourishment and energy; and since subjective concentration if applied daily will provide the brain perfectly with these two essentials, all mental troubles can be brought to an end through the art of this concentration. This is certainly a fact that will mean much, and great will be the gain to those

who apply it thoroughly. In addition to subjective concentration upon the brain, a similar
concentration should be directed every day upon
the body. This will keep the entire system balanced and strong, and will constantly create new
avenues for the upbuilding of the entire personality. Every cell in the human person contains the
possibility of a new group of cells of a higher
order which when formed will supply the requisite
channels through which a higher expression of
mind and soul may be promoted. The art of cell
building in the brain or body is therefore an art
we should all cultivate to the very highest degree.
When we concentrate daily upon all parts of the
brain, every form of mental sluggishness will
disappear, and activity will be steadily increased
in every cell. But in the increase of life and
action in the brain, we must never lose sight of
the idea of perfect poise. When we give high,
strong, well poised activity to every part of the
brain, the mind will secure an instrument through
which the greater things we have in view will
positively be accomplished.

What Is Needed—In this connection it is well
to repeat and emphasize the fact that in the development of ability along any line, there are
three principles involved. First, the number of
brain cells must be increased in that part of the
brain through which the faculty in question func-

tions. Second, the quality of the mind and the faculty must be improved. And third, the power back of the mind must be made much stronger. In other words, we must have size, quality and power, and these must be properly combined if we are to have the best results. Size, however, does not mean quantity alone, because when any part of the brain is made larger, we should also aim to make the substance of that part much finer. The more cells you can build in a given cubic inch of brain matter and the more delicate you can make the structure of those cells, the greater becomes the capacity of that part of the brain. The smaller the cells of the brain, the finer the brain. Common brain matter has large cells, and the structure of such cells is nearly always crude. The higher order of brain matter always has small cells with a fine delicate structure, and their number to each given amount of space is very large. In consequence when we proceed to develop the brain, the brain itself should be made somewhat larger. The cells should be smaller and more numerous, and the brain matter itself should be more delicate as to substance and texture. Very fine brain matter approaches the ethereal in essence and reminds you of the petals of flowers instead of crude clay. In the development of ability, the brain must receive special attention, because it is the vehicle or the instrument or the tool that the mind employs. Not that the tool is more important than the workman, but the tool in most cases has been neglected. We have tried to improve our minds and have succeeded to some extent; but we have given practically no attention to the scientific development of the brain. We have left the brain as it is and have expected the mind to do its best under such circumstances. That only a few in every age have really acquired greatness is therefore a matter that is easily explained.

All Faculties Localized—It has been thoroughly demonstrated that every talent employs one or more distinct parts of the brain, and that the development of these parts of the brain will increase the capacity and the efficiency of the talent. Consequently, when we know what part of the brain each special talent employs, the development of any talent becomes a matter of simplicity, and is placed within easy reach of everyone. As we proceed to take a general view of this idea of localization, we find that the lower half of the forehead is employed by the scientific and the practical functions of mind, and that the development of this part of the brain will increase one's ability to apply in practice what has been learned. The same development will give method, system and the happy application in the world of details. The man whose mind and brain are well developed in this region has the power to do things. He may not always have the best plans or the best methods, but he always produces results. To develop this part of the brain, concentrate attention first upon the brain center, which is a point just midway between the ears; then gradually move attention towards the lower half of the forehead until you concentrate subjectively upon all the brain matter that lies between the brain center and the lower half of the forehead. All the cells that are found in this region are concerned in the function of application. Therefore, when you concentrate, do not simply give your attention to the surface of the brain, but to the whole of that part of the brain that lies between the surface in question and the brain center.

Thought of Expansion—Another very important idea to remember is that all such concentration must contain the thought of expansion, and must be very gentle, though deep and strong. The necessity of finer consciousness while concentration is taking place must never be overlooked. For this reason we should enter into this finer consciousness before we begin. Such concentration upon any part of the brain for promoting development may last ten or fifteen minutes, and may be repeated several times a day. In your work it is a very good plan to concentrate mildly, but constantly upon that part of the brain that you use in your work; thus development will go on steadily while you are engaged in other efforts.

Pure Intellect—The upper half of the forehead is employed by the function of pure intellect. Therefore, if we wish to increase intelligence, the power of reason, understanding and intellectual capabilities in general, that part of the brain should be developed. And again we must bear in mind that it is not simply the surface that should be developed, but all the convolutions that lie between the surface and the brain center. The function of pure intellect occupies all that part of the brain that is found between the brain center and the upper half of the forehead; concentration, therefore, for the development of intellect must be directed upon all the cells found in this region. To help give quality to the intelligence you seek to perfect, try to enter into the real meaning of intelligence while you are concentrating upon this part of the brain. Try to realize as deeply as possible the true significance of intellect, and what it means to reason and understand. You will thus find that results will increase decidedly. At first, you may not gain any considerable insight into the depths of intellect, but by trying to form the most perfect conceptions of intelligence while concentrating in this manner, the brain will actually become more lucid. Your comprehension will enlarge its scope and the intellect will become more brilliant. If you have some deep subject under consideration, and you do not quite succeed in penetrating its depths, you will find the solution coming almost of itself, if you concentrate in this manner upon the upper half of the forehead while that subject is being analyzed. Perplexing problems can be solved in the same way, although the method will have to be carried out properly; that is, all the essentials involved must be given due attention. We find that we can, therefore, in this way make our intellects more brilliant than usual when occasions so demand. And we can, by daily practice, so improve intellect that we may ere long be able to understand perfectly almost any subject that is brought before our attention.

To Develop Individuality—One of the greatest faculties possessed by man is that of individuality, because it gives not only stability to what he is doing, but also causes the individual to be himself, which is highly important. No one can do his best and become all that he is capable of unless he is himself under all circumstances; and this desired trait is invariably brought out through individuality. To develop individuality, you must increase the size and the quality of that part of the brain through which it functions. And this part is illustrated in Fig. II. Individuality includes self-confidence, firmness, stability, faith and the faculty of keeping on. Thousands of fine minds fail because they do not continue right on regardless of what happens. In most instances, however, they cannot help it, because they lack individuality. We all can develop individuality, however, and we must if we wish to succeed in every undertaking for which we are fitted. To develop this faculty, concentrate upon that part of the brain indicated, and animate your concentration with a firm, self-possessed attitude of mind. In brief, as you concentrate, try to feel that you are a strong, masterful individuality, absolute monarch of your own domain. Feel that you have the power to be and do what you want to be and do, and realize that you as an individuality constitute the power that is back of and above everything that transpires in your own life. In addition to this, add faith; that is, have unbounded faith in your own individuality, and believe thoroughly that the purpose you have in view can positively be realized.

Energy and Push—The lower half of the back brain is the seat of energy, and when this is well developed we have what may be called push; that is, we will not give up our efforts because there is too much power back of those efforts. When individuality is well developed, we continue because we know that we can; and when a great deal of power is added to individuality and self-confidence, nothing can induce us to give up what we feel can be successfully pushed through. A great many people feel conditions of weakness at times, and even pain in the back brain whenever they try to push through something of importance, and the cause is lack of energy. It is therefore well to give this part of the brain attention, before we undertake any kind of work that requires a great deal of energy and perseverance. And when we feel exhaustion in the back brain, we can produce perfect relief almost at once by gently concentrating upon that part while trying at the same time to feel the presence of the finer creative energies. The development of the back brain is promoted in the same way as that of other parts with this exception: During subjective concentration upon the back of the brain, the attitude of mind must contain the thought of greater power, and you must try to feel that creative energies are accumulating more and more where your attention is directed.

Insight and Judgment—A faculty of remarkable value is that of insight or real judgment, and its place of expression is found in that part of the forehead where the cranium begins to recede. To develop this part of the brain, that is, all the brain cells that lie between the brain center and the surface of the region indicated, the process is as usual, and the mental attitude should be that of

interior insight. In other words, try to exercise
the power of interior insight in connection with
everything that you may be thinking of while concentrating for the development of this faculty.
We all come to places at times where we have to
make some important decision, but frequently we
are uncertain as to what course to pursue. Thousands have under such circumstances taken the
wrong path, and thousands in the midst of many
opportunities have selected the least because they
have no power of knowing which was the best.
Mistakes have been made without number because
we did not possess the judgment to know what
was right at the time, and a number of similar
conditions could be mentioned all arising from
the same deficiency. The development, therefore,
of judgment, discernment and insight is of more
than usual importance. When two opportunities
present themselves there ought to be something
that could inform us as to the nature of each one.
There ought to be a way to know when to do
things, when to act, which course to pursue, and
what plan to adopt. There ought to be such a
way and there is. We have the faculty of judging
these things properly. And when this faculty
is well developed, our decisions and selections will
always be the best. To proceed with the development of this faculty, the following method may
be adopted: When you have something to decide,

something of great importance, but do not know what decision to make, do not think of the matter for the time being, but proceed instead to give special attention to this faculty of insight. Concentrate subjectively at frequent intervals upon the brain cells involved. Try to increase their number; refine the substance of which they are composed, and try to give the faculty of judgment and decision the most perfect vehicle of expression possible. Continue this for a few hours or a few days if you can put off the decision that long. Then take up the problem and try to see the best way. If the faculty in question is sufficiently awakened, you will know almost at once what course to pursue, and you will lose all desire for other plans. But should you fail to receive a decided answer, let the problem go for a while longer, and proceed to awaken this faculty still further. You will soon bring this faculty up to the desired state of lucidity, and the decision will be made. In addition to this method, carry on regular development every day as you do with all your other faculties.

Improvement of Quality—We gain size in any faculty through the use of subjective concentration, but quality and power are developed in other ways. The first essential in the production of quality consists of forming the highest mental conceptions possible of the faculties themselves as well as every thought or idea that may enter the mind. The term "mental conception" simply means the idea that you form of anything of which you may be thinking. Every idea you form in mind is a mental concept and it serves as a vital factor in the upbuilding of the talent you h a v e u n d e r consideration. Metaphysically speaking, every idea is composed of the ideas which you have formed concerning that talent, and every faculty is as large and as perfect as your conscious or interior understanding of the function of that faculty. Therefore, the more perfectly you understand the inner life, the soul, the essence, the true nature, the scope and the possibilities of a talent, the higher will be your mental conceptions of that talent. And the higher these conceptions are the higher will be the quality of the talent itself. To state this matter more simply, we might say that the first law in the improvement of quality among the faculties of the mind, is to have as great and as lofty thoughts as possible at all times. To carry out this idea, we should hold our minds in the loftiest attitude possible whenever we concentrate for the development of any part of the brain. Thus we will develop mental quality at the same time as we develop brain capacity. When we concentrate attention upon the upper half of the forehead, we should hold in mind at the time the highest, the broadest and the deepest conceptions of pure intellect that we can form. The result of this dual process will be increased quality in our intelligence and a more perfect brain through which this improved intellect may be expressed. In promoting development along other lines, the same idea should be applied, and we may thus secure results along several lines through every individual process.

Increase of Power—The first step in the increase of power is to preserve the energies we already possess. There is an enormous amount of energy generated in the average personality, but the larger part of this is usually wasted. Therefore, if we simply prevented this waste, we should, in many instances, have more energy than we could use, no matter along how many lines we wish to promote development. To prevent this waste of energy, all discord must be avoided and perfect poise attained; there must be no anger, no worry, no despondency and no fear; the mind must be composed, the nervous system in harmony and the entire personality in tune with the serenity of the soul. When this has been accomplished, we shall feel a great deal stronger both in mind and body.

Important Fact—We shall realize a decided increase in the force and energy throughout every part of our systems. The personality will feel as if it were charged, so to speak, with energies we never felt before, and we realize that we have come into possession of new and stronger forces than we have ever supposed in the past. When this accumulation of energy is felt, however, we should not become too enthusiastic nor too determined, as such a course may tend to destroy our poise, and thus produce the waste we have tried to avoid. Instead these great moments should be employed in gently directing attention towards those parts of the brain and the mind that we wish to develop. In this way we will give added power to the building up of any particular talent towards which we may be giving our attention; but when our minds become so large that we require more energy than what is being generated in our systems now, we shall find it necessary to secure an additional supply; and this is done by awakening the great within; that is by directing the subconscious to give expression to more and more energy as we may require.

Transmutation—In the increase and use of creative energy, the process of transmutation becomes absolutely necessary; and to transmute any force in the system means to change that force from a lower to a higher state of action; or to change any creative power from its present purpose to some other purpose than we may have in mind. To change any force to a higher or finer state of action, we should enter into the conscious feeling of the finer forces of the system. And this is not difficult as anyone will find after making a few attempts along this line. Through the process of transmutation, all the forces of the system at any time can be changed to different forces, and can be gathered for special work in that part of the system where special development is to take place. The value of transmutation, therefore, is very great, and should receive thorough and constant attention.

Added Lines of Expression—Whenever the creative forces accumulate, the predominating thought held in mind at the time becomes the pattern, and what the creative forces produce will always be similar to the nature of this predominating thought. Therefore, when we concentrate upon any part of the brain for the purpose of development, the thought of development, expansion and growth should receive our first attention. This practice will aid remarkably in the increase of brain cells, and as each brain cell is a channel of expression for the conscious action of that talent that functions through the part in question, we realize its great value. The more brain cells there are in a given place, the more channels of expression will be secured for that talent; and the more channels of expression we provide for a talent, the greater the capacity and power of that talent. To help increase the number of cells in any part of the brain, all the essentials of the talent that function through that part should be held in consciousness during such concentration. And the essentials of a talent are all those different parts of the talent that one can become conscious of by trying to examine that talent from every possible point of view. The more essentials or actions of the talent we are conscious of while we concentrate upon any part of the brain, the more lines of expression we will produce in that part. And since each line of expression tends to create its own cell, provided there is sufficient nourishment and energy in that particular place, the number of brain cells will necessarily increase in proportion to the number of essentials we hold in mind during the process of concentration.

Multiplication of Ideas—In the beginning all that is necessary is to have a clear idea of the nature of the talent you wish to develop, and then hold that clear idea in mind during concentration. As you proceed, this idea will subdivide again and again until it becomes a score of ideas, and each of these ideas will become an essential, that is, a distinct part of the talent and an individual line of action for that talent. You realize, therefore, that to see all the essentials of a talent with the mind's eye, is to dissect that talent and see all its parts as parts, and how they are united to form the one talent. The value of this process is found in the fact that the more parts of the talent you are conscious of while concentrating, the more cells you will create in that part of the brain upon which you concentrate, provided, you hold in mind very clearly the principal ideas of the talent that functions through that particular part. Another gain from the same process is found in the fact that it tends to increase the channels of expression for the talent itself. And the more channels of expression we provide for a talent, the greater that talent becomes.

The Brain Center—When concentrating upon any part of the brain, we should always begin at the brain center; that is, where all the lines meet as indicated in Figure II. We should begin by drawing all the forces of the mind towards this center, and when we feel that consciousness is concentrated, so to speak, at this point, we should turn attention upon that part of the brain we wish to develop. Then we should concentrate upon the entire region from the brain center to the surface of the cranium as it is all the cells within that space that we wish to multiply, refine and develop.

The Metaphysical Side—That part of the brain marked "interior understanding" is employed by the metaphysical side of the mind. Through this region the mind discerns the interior and higher aspects of life, and is therefore of great importance. When this part of the brain lacks in development the mind sees only the surface of things, and the deeper things of life are therefore beyond his understanding. But since the attainment of real worth depends upon our ability to understand the inner and real side of things, this part of the brain must never be neglected. When we concentrate upon this region we should open the mind fully to thought from the depths of consciousness. We should begin by turning all attention away from things and external ideas, and think only of the most perfect ideas that we can form of everything of which we are conscious. It is not necessary to attempt any profound analysis of the abstract, but simply to hold attention upon that perfect something that permeates everything. We should not at this time think of flaws, defects, mistakes or imperfections, but should hold the idea of absolute perfection uppermost in mind. The possibility of absolute perfection is a matter we need not discuss with ourselves because we know that there is such a thing. It is upon our most perfect idea of the perfect that we should turn attention. In the development of this faculty we should remember that there is such a thing as metaphysical consciousness, a consciousness that is distinct from intellectual understanding, and the distinction is this, that the intellectual understanding understands how things are related to each other, while this inner metaphysical understanding understands the things themselves. The intellectual understands phenomena. The interior understands that which produces the phenomena. It is this metaphysical consciousness or understanding that we should seek to realize when we concentrate for the development of this region of the brain. Therefore, all thought must be directed upon the perfect; that is, that something that we discern when metaphysical consciousness begins. The real value of this consciousness will be more fully realized when we come to study special talents, as we shall then find that every talent has a metaphysical foundation, and that to perfect the quality and true worth of that talent we must express more fully the metaphysical nature of that talent. But since we cannot increase the expression of anything until we become conscious of it, we realize that metaphysical consciousness becomes indispensable to those who wish to grow in genuine quality and true worth.

The Use of Emotion—That region of the brain marked "emotion" is the channel of sympathy and every tender feeling of mind or soul. It is through the functions that employ this region that the mind finds unity and at-one-ment with everything that exists; and as the realization of unity and harmony with all things is absolutely necessary to the highest development of mind, this faculty should be well developed. In a great many people the emotional side is more or less perverted, and takes the form of sentimentalism. But this does not come from an over-development of this faculty. On the contrary, it is due to a false conception of the finer things in life, and is therefore caused principally by the lack of intelligence. In concentrating upon this part of the brain, the purpose should be the development of a larger channel for the expression of true sympathy. Everything should occupy the foremost place in mind at the time. But when we think of sympathy, we should think of it as being the essence of the highest unity conceivable, and not as a mere mode of sympathizing with people. When the average person sympathizes, he usually comes down and feels like those with whom he sympathizes; he does not try to realize that finer and higher unity that exists among all things. Therefore he is not in sympathy. He simply imitates the emotions of the other person, and this is a violation of all the laws of man. To feel that deep and high unity that makes all creation one is the purpose of sympathy, and when we feel this sublime unity, we become conscious of the most beautiful and the most tender emotions that the soul can possibly know. Accordingly, the value of such development becomes two-fold; first, the most beautiful qualities of life are brought into expression; and second the mind learns to view all things from that higher state of consciousness where the unity and the harmony of all is discerned. And here we find the secret of knowing the truth, because to know the truth is to see all things from the viewpoint of unity; it is to stand at that place from which all things proceed and to see clearly what they are, where they are going, and what their purpose in life or action happens to be. True sympathy, or the realization of the finer emotion, will tend to bring the mind to this place, because all these high emotions will draw irresistibly upon the mind, thereby leading consciousness up to that place where perfect unity is absolutely real. We all know that the finest emotions of the soul constantly lead us towards higher places. And we also know that the higher we go in consciousness the more perfect becomes our understanding of all things. The value of sympathy, therefore, in its true sense is very great indeed.

The Power of Intuition—The most successful men in the world have had the faculty of intuition developed to a high degree and have thus been able to take advantage of the best opportunities at the proper time. History is full of incidents where men and women have arisen to high places by following the indications of this great faculty. It gives the mind the power to see through things as they are and therefore reveals, not only the facts in the case, but also indicates how to deal with those facts. Intuition may work consciously or unconsciously, but whenever it is well developed it works, and works well. As previously stated, we may develop this faculty by concentrating subjectively at frequent intervals every day upon that part of the brain indicated in Figure II, and we should, during the process of concentration give our attention to the idea of interior insight; that is, we should try to see through things and try to know directly or at first hand without resorting to reason or analysis. In this connection a strong desire for deeper discernment is of the highest value if such desire is expressed persistently whenever we concentrate for development. The development of this faculty can be promoted decidedly by making it a point to have more and more faith in its judgment, and also by depending upon it for judgment in every case that comes up. Like all other things, it developes through use if that use is thorough and continuous. It is a splendid practice to make it a point never to decide upon anything without first getting the highest possible light of intuition on the subject, and also to have perfect faith in your ability to get the real truth in this way. Through this practice you will give more and more energy and life to this faculty. And accordingly it will develop steadily and surely until it becomes sufficiently developed to express its function even to a remarkable degree.

The Most Important Faculty—All the faculties of the mind are important and necessary to each other, but the most important of all is unquestionably that of intellect. This faculty, therefore, should receive our first attention unless it is already well developed. Through the proper concentration upon that part of the brain that is employed by the intellect, remarkable intelligence can possibly be developed, and results will appear at the very beginning. The very first time you concentrate upon that part of the brain with the thought of brilliancy in mind you realize that your mentality becomes clearer and more lucid; you can think better; fine thoughts come more readily, and you can understand things with a clearness that is sometimes remarkable. You do not simply think that the improvement has been realized, however, because in dealing with difficult problems you actually demonstrate that the lucidity of your mind has been decidedly improved. To promote this development we should concentrate attention upon the upper half of the

forehead whenever we think or study, as we shall
in this way increase the capacity of intelligence
at the very time when we are making direct use
of it; and we shall accordingly have better results both in our thinking, or study, and in our development. But all such concentration should
be easy, and should be associated with the consciousness of the finer creative energies. When
you feel the action of these finer forces, you do
not have to compel them to work. They work
easily, smoothly and harmoniously of their own
accord when placed in action. In fact, they act
and work as if directed by some superior power;
and this is really true because when you awaken
the higher powers within you, you are actually
bringing into action powers that are superior,
powers that have no limitations whatever.

Application and Expression—That region of
the brain that is marked "application" is employed by the mind in the doing of things; that is,
those faculties that express themselves through
this region have the power to use what we understand, and therefore unites intellect with the
world of things. When we develop this faculty
we shall find that it is just as easy to practice as
to theorize, and that every idea of value can be
turned to practical use in the tangible world.
When trying to develop this faculty, we should
hold in mind thoughts of system, method and

scientific application. And we should try to feel that we are consciously related to all things in the outer world. Then, to this attitude we should add a strong desire to do things and achieve much, and we shall find ourselves laying the foundation for a power of application that will be a practical power indeed. Through this same region we find the action of the faculty of expression, and though this faculty is employed largely in connection with musical, artistic and literary talents, it is by no means confined to those talents. The power of expression, generally speaking, is used by all faculties and is absolutely necessary to everybody in bringing forth what there is in them. When we develop the power of expression we tend to bring forth our own individuality and make the personality far more powerful than it has been before. And in addition all the talents we employ will express themselves with more thoroughness, efficiency and power. For general purposes we should concentrate upon this part of the brain in the attitude of a strong desire for full expression of mind, soul and personality. And we should try to feel at the time that every power or faculty in our possession is being expressed more and more through its own channel.

Perseverance and Enthusiasm—In all concentration for development we should give the most time to those faculties that we need in our work, and especially to those that are weak and inferior. Our object should be to secure a well developed brain in all respects, and to give special development to those faculties that we use in our vocation. When concentrating upon a certain part of the brain we should think only of that talent or faculty that functions through that part, and we should try to realize as fully as possible the interior or potential nature of that talent. To think of the unlimited possibilities that exist within the talent is of the highest value during concentration, because in this way the richest thought that we are capable of creating will be introduced into the process of development. In all these efforts perservance and enthusiasm are indispensable. Principles must be applied and to all such application we should give our whole life and soul. The first essential is to understand the principles of mind development. And the second is to persevere in every application, giving so much enthusiasm to all our efforts that every element and force within us is called to action. It is in this way, and in this way alone, that results will be secured, and when we persevere in this manner results will positively be secured. The amount of time that will be required to secure decided results will depend upon our own efforts. To develop ability or genius up to a high state will require years, but in the meantime, we shall be gaining ground steadily. And so long as we are steadily improving we know that we shall finally reach the goal in view, no matter how high or how wonderful that goal may be. Anyone, however, who will faithfully apply the above principles as well as the other principles presented in this study, will realize a decided improvement from the very beginning, and may secure even remarkable results in a few months time. In fact, the majority of those who take up this study should at least double their mental power and ability every year, and a large percentage will positively do far better than this.

CHAPTER VI

SPECIAL BRAIN DEVELOPMENT

The Eight Principal Divisions—That every faculty of the mind functions through one or more distinct parts of the brain is no longer mere theory; it is a fact that leading scientists of the world are demonstrating to be true. And that any part of the brain can be developed through the art of subjective concentration, is also a fact that is being conclusively demonstrated at the present time. It is therefore evident that when we know exactly through what part of the brain each faculty functions, we can increase the power and the efficiency of that faculty to any degree desired, provided we develop the mental faculty itself as well as that part of the brain through which it functions. It is with the development of the brain that we are now concerned, however, because this phase has been entirely neglected by all previous systems of mental training. In Fig. IV we present the eight principal divisions of the brain, although these divisions do not represent the same number of individual faculties. On the contrary, a group of faculties function through each division, but in each case the individual faculties of any one group are so closely related that they can be developed together. Thus time is saved, and a more thorough development is secured.

The Practical Brain—That part of the brain that is marked No. 1 in Fig. IV may be very appropriately termed the practical brain, as it is through this part that the mind functions when direct practical action is being expressed. Whenever you try to be practical your mind begins at once to act upon the practical brain, and when the practical brain is well developed you are naturally of a practical turn of mind. The practical brain should be developed by everybody, and especially by those who are engaged in vocations where system, method and the mastery of details are required. Concentrate subjectively upon this part of the brain for a few minutes several times a day, and whenever you are engaged in the actual doing of things, think of the practical brain; that is, aim to focus the power of thought, attention and application upon this part of the brain, and aim to act through the practical brain whenever you apply yourself practically.

The Mechanical Brain—Every building process and all the faculties of construction function through the mechanical brain (See No. 2, Fig. IV). Engineers, mechanics and builders of every description should develop this part of the brain; and these are the two methods that may be employed. First, use subjective concentration whenever you have a few moments to spare; and second, train your mind to work through the mechanical brain while you are engaged in your special line of constructive work. When you are laying bricks, do not think at random; think of improving your skill; and as you think, try to turn the full power of your thought into the mechanical brain. The power of your mind, instead of being aimlessly scattered, will thus accumulate in the mechanical brain, and will daily strengthen, develop and build up that part of the brain. In the course of time you will become a mechanical genius, and scores of valuable opportunities will be opened for you. If you are building a bridge, digging a tunnel, running an engine or working on some invention, apply the same principle. Train your mind to act directly upon the mechanical brain while you are at work, and deeply desire the active powers of your mind to steadily build up that part of the brain. You will soon become an expert in your line of work, and later on a genius.

The Financial Brain—We all need a very good development of the financial brain (See No. 3, Fig. IV), because the full value of life cannot be gained so long as there is the slightest trace of poverty. When the financial brain is so well developed as to balance properly with all the other leading faculties, the use of those other faculties will result in financial gain; but where the financial brain is weak and small, financial gains will be meager, even though there may be extraordinary ability along other lines. No matter how remarkable your talents may be along any special line, you will not make much money through the use of those talents unless your financial brain is well developed; but if this part of the brain is exceptionally developed, everything you touch will be turned to money. The making of money, however, is not the sole purpose of life; the making of money will not, in itself, produce happiness, nor make living worth while, but it is a necessary part of the real purpose of life; therefore everybody should develop the financial brain to a good degree. If you are not directly connected with the financial world, give your financial brain a few moments attention, through subjective concentration, every day; that will prove sufficient. And as you concentrate, think of accumulation, desire accumulation, and try to feel that you are in the process of accumulation. But if you are engaged directly in the financial world, whether in banking, brokerage, financial management, financial promotion or in any form of actual financial work whatever, give your financial brain thorough development.   Aim to work through this brain, and use subjective concentration for a few minutes every hour if possible.

The Executive Brain—That part of the brain marked "4" in Fig. IV is employed by the mind in all forms of management.   Those who govern, rule, manage, superintend or occupy positions at the head of enterprises, should give special attention to the development of the executive brain. When this part of the brain is large, strong and well developed, we possess what is termed "backbone"; and we have real, substantial "backing" for every purpose, plan or idea that we may wish to carry through.   We have force and determination, and have the power as well as the "knack" of guiding the ship of any enterprise through the storms of every obstacle, adversity or difficulty, to a safe landing, at the haven of great success.   The true executive governs perfectly without giving anyone the impression that he is trying to rule; he governs, not by personal force, but by superior leadership; he has the power that can rule, therefore does not have to try to rule.   The strong man never domineers; it is only weak men who would like to rule that ever domineer; but it is time and energy wasted. Never try to domineer over anything or try to forcefully rule anybody if you would attain superior executive power.   To develop the executive brain, try to realize the position and power of true leadership whenever you apply subjective concentration in that part, or apply executive power in daily life. Aim to make the executive brain as large and strong as possible, and whenever you use the executive faculty, try to feel that it is the executive brain that gives the necessary power.

The Volitional Brain—The development of the fifth division of the brain produces will power, personal force, determination, push, perseverance, persistence, self-confidence, firmness and self-control. When the volitional brain is well developed you are no longer a part of the mass; you stand out as a distinct individuality, and you are a special power in the world in which you work and live. The volitional brain, therefore, should be thoroughly developed by every mind that aims to become something more than a mere cog in the industrial machine. The best way to proceed with this development is to concentrate subjectively upon the volitional brain for ten or fifteen minutes every morning. This will give you the power to control more fully your thought, your actions and your circumstances during the day. When you concentrate hold yourself in the attitude of self-control, and deeply will with all the power of will that you possess. Whenever you are called upon to use exceptional will-power or "stand your ground" against temptations or adverse circumstances, turn your attention upon the volitional brain; that is, think of the volitional brain when you use your will, your determination or your self-control, and you will feel yourself becoming stronger and stronger in personal power and will-power until nothing in the world can cause you to budge in the least from the true position you have taken.

The Aspiring Brain—When the mind aspires toward the ideal, the beautiful, the sublime, the actions of the mind function through that part of the brain designated in the sixth division in Fig. IV. When you "hitch your wagon to a star" you act through the aspiring brain; you do the same when you feel ambitious, or express real desire for higher attainments and greater achievements. It is the aspiring brain that prompts you to advance, to improve yourself, to push to the front, to do great things in the world, to live a life worth while; and it is the same brain that keeps you in touch with the greater possibilities that exist in every conceivable field of action. Develop the aspiring brain and you will become ambitions; you will gain a strong desire to rise out of the common; all the tendencies of your mind will begin to move toward greater things; you will discern the ideal; you will begin to have

visions of extraordinary attainments and achievements, and you will be inspired with an "upward
and onward force" that will give you no peace
until you begin to work in earnest to make your
lofty dreams come true.   So long as the aspiring brain is small and weak, you will have neither
the power nor the desire to get above mere, common existence; but when this part of the brain
becomes large, strong and thoroughly developed,
you will have the power and the desire to reach
the top; and to the top you will positively go.   To
develop this part of the brain two things are necessary.   Concentrate subjectively upon the aspiring brain whenever you have a few moments to
spare, and during every moment of such concentration, "Hitch your wagon to a star."

The Imaging Brain—This part of the brain
(See No. 7, Fig. IV) may be properly termed the
"idea factory."   It is the imaging brain that
creates ideas, that forms plans, that formulates
methods and that combines, adjusts and read-
justs the various elements that are embraced in
whatever the mind may create.   To accomplish
greater things we must have greater ideas, more
extensive plans and more perfect methods.   The
imaging faculty can furnish all three precisely
as we may desire, provided the imaging brain
is developed to higher and higher degrees.   To

proceed, turn your attention upon the imaging brain whenever you use your imagination or whenever you picture anything in your mind. When you are in search of new ideas, look into the imaging brain, and use subjective concentration in arousing this part of the brain to higher and finer activity. Think with the imaging brain whenever you are engaged in forming new plans or formulating new methods, and always aim to express the expansive attitude through that part of the brain. In other words, when you use the imaging or concentrate subjectively upon that part of the brain, think of the imaging faculty as expanding into larger and greater fields of thought. Your mental creative power will thus become greater and greater; you will grasp a much larger world of thought, action and possibility, and the superior ideas and plans desired will soon be secured.

The Intellectual Brain—The eighth division of the brain, as illustrated in Figure IV, is the seat of pure intelligence, reason, judgment, analysis, conception and understanding. Every cell in the brain is animated with intelligence, because intelligence is an attribute of every faculty of the mind, but it is through the intellectual brain that the mind functions when it thinks with that form of intelligence that not only knows, but knows that

it knows. Whenever you attempt to understand
any particular subject or object, turn your attention upon the intellectual brain, and try to think
directly with that part of the brain. Do the same
when you reason about anything, when you proceed to analyze anything, or try to find the solution of any problem. Concentrate subjectively
upon the intellectual brain for a few minutes
several times a day; and while you concentrate,
try to see through every thought that comes into
your mind at the time. This will increase remarkably your power to know, and will, at
the same time, increase the general power of
your mental ability. All ability depends, to
some degree, upon the power of your intellect;
therefore, whatever your work, give special and
daily attention to the development of the intellectual brain. As the faculty of pure intellect, reason and understanding is increased
in efficiency and power, every other active
faculty in the mind will also increase in efficiency
and power. It is the intellectual brain that
guides the whole brain; and, therefore, intellectual advancement means general advancement;
but this general advancement in every part of
the brain and the mind will not be satisfactory
unless the whole of the brain is developed in proportion. Develop the intellectual brain continu-

ously, no matter what your work; give special and continuous development to that part of the brain that is employed directly in your work; and give general development to your whole brain; this is the perfect rule to follow in order to secure the proper results.

CHAPTER VII

THE INNER SECRET

In order to develop any part of the physical system, two essentials are required. The first is more nourishment in that particular part, and the second is an increase in creative energy. The circulation conveys nourishment to all parts of the system, and the nerves transmit the creative energies; therefore, wherever we increase the circulation, additional nourishment will be supplied, and wherever the activity of the nerves is increased or intensified, there creative energy will accumulate. Accordingly, the question will be how to increase the circulation wherever we like, and how to intensify the activity of any desired nerve center. Experiments, however, have demonstrated that this problem is not as difficult as it may seem, because wherever mental attention is concentrated, an increase both in the circulation and in the nerve activity takes place. But this concentration must be in the right mental attitude, and here we come to the inner secret.

It has been discovered that all functions of the personality are under the direct control of what is termed the finer subjective forces, and in order to master any physical function or mental faculty, these finer forces must be employed. Wherever these subjective forces display the greatest activity, there the circulation is the strongest, and there the creative energies naturally accumulate; and these subjective forces will display the greatest activity wherever attention is concentrated during subjective consciousness. The secret, therefore, is to enter subjective consciousness before we begin to concentrate for any desired development; and by subjective consciousness we mean that mental state wherein the finer forces of the system can be felt. But this is not something new or something difficult to attain. We all are more or less on the verge of this consciousness all the time, and most of us enter into it frequently.

When you are thrilled by music that stirs the very soul of your being you are in subjective consciousness, and it is the finer forces or interior vibrations that produce the delightful sensation you feel at the time. When you are inwardly touched by the beauties of nature, you are in this same consciousness; and it is these finer forces that create the lofty thoughts you think during such moments. There are any number of experiences that could be mentioned to illustrate what is meant by subjective consciousness, but the two just mentioned will give anyone the key. And here we must remember that it is this state that we must enter whenever we concentrate for development, either for mind, brain or body; the reason being, that while the mind is in this finer subjective state, the actions of mind will directly control the subjective forces. When the mind is in subjective consciousness, the subjective forces will follow concentration, thus drawing more creative energy and a stronger circulation to that place upon which attention is directed. This is the law, and it is just as unfailing as any law in nature. But how to take the mind into subjective consciousness at any time is of course the problem, although the solution is by no means difficult to find.

When we know what subjective consciousness really is, and remember the sensation we have felt while in such a state at previous times, we can readily transfer the mind to the field of the finer forces by simply desiring to do so, but we must not make a strenuous effort in that direction. To keep the mind upon the ideal and the more refined for a few moments is usually sufficient to awaken subjective consciousness in most instances; and to think of anything that is lofty and sublime, or that touches the soul will invariably produce the same result. In brief, anything that will cause your mind to pass from the mere surface of thought into the finer depths of life may be employed in the beginning to induce this finer state. Possibly few external helps would be better than that of listening for a few moments to sweet, tender, soulful music, and the reading of poetry that really is poetry will usually serve the same purpose. It must be remembered, however, that when we employ external aids in this connection we must make a deep, but gentle effort to enter into sympathetic touch with the soul of that which we employ at the time.

When we gain the mastery of our own consciousness we can enter the subjective state or withdraw from that state at any time as we like. In fact, we can do this just as easily as we can open or close our eyes. This mastery, therefore, should be our great object in view when we are depending upon temporary or external helps. Another method for assisting the mind in producing subjective consciousness is the study of the different planes of vibration with a view of gaining a perfect understanding of the true nature of each individual plane. This is an immense and a most interesting study, and will prove extremely valuable in mental development, for the reason that the mind can consciously enter and consciously act upon any plane that it understands. Therefore, when the mind understands the nature of subjective consciousness, it can enter that state at any time by simply deciding to do so. To gain a better understanding of the various planes of consciousness and the ascending scales of vibrations, the latest discoveries both in physical science and in psychology should be noted with the greatest of care.   The Xrays and the Nrays demonstrate conclusively the existence of finer forces and higher vibrations in nature; and the fact that every plane in nature has a corresponding plane in man has been known for a long time. It is also a well known fact that man has a higher sense or consciousness to correspond with every higher force or plane in nature.   Therefore the fact that there are higher forces in nature proves that there are higher states of consciousness in man; and it is our privilege to have all of these developed whenever we may so desire.

Many minds look upon the visible physical body as all there is of the body, but chemistry has demonstrated conclusively that within the purely physical body there exists a finer grade of elements, and within this finer grade a still finer grade and so on for a number of grades, the exact number of which has not been determined. The physical body therefore is, strictly speaking, composed of a number of forms, the outermost form being in the lowest grade of vibration, while the innermost forms being in such a high grade of vibration that they approach what scientists call ethereal elements.   Just at this point the subconscious begins and we have a vast interior world, the immensity of which will possibly never be fully demonstrated.   It is this interior world that we call "the great within," and it is the source of the boundless possibilities that are latent in man.   Whenever we are more or less in touch with this inner or finer realm we are in subjective consciousness, and it is only necessary to touch the subconscious to gain control of the finer forces.

Subjective consciousness deals with a boundless realm and therefore we may expand the mind into this vast realm perpetually, gaining mastery over greater and greater powers as we advance. In usual brain development the mere feeling of these finer forces of the subjective field is all that is necessary to secure results.   And those who employ the helps already presented will find no difficulty whatever in reaching this deeper or finer state of feeling.   When you are in subjective consciousness during concentration, you can readily feel those finer forces in that part of the brain that you are trying to develop, and you can also feel an increase in the circulation in the same place. The finer creative energies are not always as distinctly felt, but they are always present in abundance where the finer activities are at work.   When we begin to gain control of the subjective forces so that we can draw all the creative energies of the system into any part of the brain or body where we desire development, we find we are beginning to master another great process, without doubt one of the greatest processes in the being of man; in other words, what may be truthfully called the inner secret of all human development; and as we advance in the application of the principle of this secret, we shall advance in development in proportion.   But as there is no end to the possibilities of this secret, there is necessarily no end to what man may develop in his own mind and soul as he advances in the scientific use of the principle involved.

CHAPTER VIII

THE FINER FORCES

The consciousness of and the proper direction of the finer forces in mind and personality, is absolutely necessary in all development of brain or mind, and therefore we must learn to know those forces whenever their actions are felt in the system. One of the first signs of the presence of these finer forces is indicated by peculiar warmth in the deeper life of the body, especially when the forces are strong; though it is not necessary that they should produce this warmth nor that they should produce any pronounced physical sensation whatever. It is very important, however, that we learn to distinguish between the finer forces and the other forces in the system because when the finer forces are discerned they may be directed anywhere to promote development. And here we must remember that unless these finer forces are placed in action, no development can possibly take place.

The inner forces are the interior creative energies of the human personality. They are the invisible builders of every force in the body and every state, quality and faculty in the mind.

Therefore to promote growth anywhere in the human system, the action of the finer forces in that part must be increased.

When the finer forces are felt or discerned they will readily accumulate wherever attention may be directed; and wherever they accumulate there life, nourishment, vitality, and everything necessary to growth and construction, will accumulate also. To discern the finer forces it is necessary for the mind to enter into the consciousness of those elements that permeate the physical elements; that is, conscious action must act not upon the physical person, but upon the real life that thrills every atom in the person. During this conscious action no thought whatever must be given to physical matter nor must the mind dwell upon shape or form. When the mind thinks of shape, form, or physical matter during the process of concentration, attention will be directed upon physical matter instead of upon that life that gives animation to matter. The desired results therefore will not be forthcoming. To arouse the finer forces, attention must be concentrated upon those forces; the mind must think of those forces, and consciousness must seek to enter into the very life of those forces. This, however, is not possible while one is thinking of the body or giving attention to its shape and form.

To develop any part of the brain, the cells in that part should be made more refined and more numerous. To accomplish this, more energy, more life and more nourishment will be needed in the part to be developed; and all of these will accumulate where desired if the finer forces are active in the system, and attention is concentrated upon the exact place where development is to take place. During this concentration, however, no thought must be given to the physical brain cells. Attention must be devoted exclusively to the finer elements, the finer forces, the finer life that permeates the finer forces, and the finer life that permeates the physical cells.

Concentrate attention upon the finer forces in any part of the system, and those forces from any part of the system will accumulate at the point of concentration; and whatever you desire to develop at the time, those forces will proceed to develop. When this accumulation of the finer forces or energies is taking place, their presence can sometimes be felt, and they produce a very delicate vibratory sensation. Sometimes these vibrations produce electric thrills, a sensation that is most delightful, and sometimes they cause the personality to feel, as it were, a living magnet, which is true. When the finer forces are highly active, the personality actually becomes a living magnet and gains at the time the creative power of rare genius.

The actions and the vibrations of the finer forces never feel as if they were on the surface, nor even in an external state of physical substance. On the contrary, they always feel as if they were deeply permeating physical substance, giving external power, so to speak, to external shape and form. To try to feel the finer forces, however, is not desirable. Our purpose is to arouse them into high and full action, and whenever they are in action, we shall feel them without trying to do so. When we try to feel those forces, the mind will give its attention to sensation, and sensation is simply effect; but to produce the action of those forces as well as the feeling of their presence in the system, we must act upon those forces themselves; that is, we must act upon the cause, and whenever we produce the desired cause, the desired effect will invariably follow.

CHAPTER IX

SUBJECTIVE CONCENTRATION

To concentrate upon the finer essence, the finer life of the finer forces in any part of the brain, or in any part of the personality, is termed subjective concentration, and there is no other form of concentration that has any value for any purpose whatever. To accomplish anything in any field of action, concentration is indispensable, but that concentration must be subjective to produce results. And to concentrate subjectively is to act mentally in the conscious feeling of that finer life, essence or force that permeates the objective or physical life.

There are two sides to the human system, the objective and the subjective. The objective is the external, the tangible or the physical side. The subjective is the interior, the finer, or the metaphysical side. The subjective permeates the objective. The metaphysical or the subjective is the cause, or constitutes the realm of cause, and therefore controls the physical, and determines every effect that will be produced in the physical. For this reason, the mind must concentrate upon the metaphysical and produce the desired cause in the metaphysical in order to secure any desired effect or result in the physical. It is the finer metaphysical forces that control the vital forces and the chemical forces in the body, and it is these same forces that are usually termed creative energies. It is these that create and develop, and therefore to promote development, these finer forces must be awakened, directed and properly applied.

To awaken the finer forces of the system, the mind must concentrate attention upon the finer essence or substance that permeates the physical substance of the personality, and this is accomplished by trying to feel the finer forces while the mind is thinking deeply of the subjective or finer life of the system. The principle is this, that the substance of which the body is composed is actually permeated with a much finer substance, just as water permeates a sponge, and that this finer substance or essence is filled with forces that are much finer and far more rapid than the ordinary physical forces. To concentrate subjectively is to direct attention upon this finer essence and these finer forces, and when the mind actually succeeds in acting upon this finer essence the finer forces of the system will be placed in action.

Wherever these forces begin to act, there development will take place. Therefore, to promote development in any part of the brain or in any part of the personality all that is necessary is to concentrate subjectively on that part, and have clearly fixed in mind at the time the degree of development that is desired. To concentrate upon the finer essence of the brain center is to think about the finer substance that permeates the physical brain center, and then turn attention upon that finer substance. In this way the finer forces of the brain will be acted upon, and when these forces are acted upon they will do whatever the mind may desire to have done at the time.

What to think while concentrating subjectively depends upon what one desires to develop, attain or accomplish through such concentration. And this can be determined by applying the principle of scientific thinking. The most important principle in scientific thinking is to think only of that now that you are trying to accomplish now, and turn all the power of thought, life, consciousness and attention upon that one subject. And here we must realize that without scientific thinking concentration is of no value; in fact, it ceases to be concentration; because to try to concentrate upon one subject while thinking of something else is a mere scattering of force. When concentrating upon a certain faculty one should think about the more perfect state of that faculty and also what one desires to accomplish through the use of that faculty. In this connection the construc-

tive use of the imagination will prove highly
profitable, because what is imagined in the mind
during any process of subjective concentration
will be created and developed in the mind. What
is imaged in the mind when concentration is
not subjective, will not be developed in the mind,
because the creative forces, those forces that
develop, are not brought into action unless concentration is subjective. To awaken these forces
attention must act in the subjective field of consciousness; and this field is simply a field of finer
life and action permeating every part of the
human system.

To enter mentally into this finer field is not difficult. In fact, when anyone feels deeply, the
mind is more or less in the subjective. The same
is true when attention enters an attitude of deep,
whole-souled interest, a fact that can easily be
demonstrated because concentration is always
perfect when the interest is absolute; and a finer,
stronger life is always felt at such times. Whenever a person concentrates with a deep, living
interest, he concentrates subjectively, and if he
would analyze the experience he would find that
he was not interested in the outer phase of the
subject, but actually entered into the real interior
life of the subject itself. The simple principle is
that when we enter into a subject we concentrate
subjectively upon that subject. And when we

enter into the finer essence or life of an object, we concentrate subjectively upon that object. The process of subjective concentration, therefore, is easily understood and applied. It is not something special that we have to learn because we are concentrating subjectively more or less all the time, that is, whenever we direct attention upon anything with a deep, living interest. It is a process, however, that should be developed thoroughly and completely mastered as it constitutes the principal secret to all attainment and achievement.

CHAPTER X

PRINCIPLE OF CONCENTRATION

To do one thing at a time and to give one's whole thought and attention to what is being done now is the principle upon which concentration is based, and nothing worth while can be accomplished without concentration. This principle, however, is not confined to definite lines of action, nor does it necessarily mean that the well concentrated mind moves in a groove. On the contrary, the more perfect the power of concentration, the more easily can the mind turn its attention with full force to any subject or object that may be considered. To be able to concentrate well does not simply mean to be able to give one's whole attention to present action; it also means the power to turn one's complete attention upon any new subject or object at will.

In the first place, concentration is a function of the conscious mind only. It is not necessary to concentrate upon that which the subconscious is doing; and all the automatic actions of mind or body are directed by the subconscious; that is, after the subconscious has been given the proper directions, no further concentration along those

lines will be necessary.   It is only such actions as
have not been given definite tendencies and such
modes of thought or effort as require special
attention, that need concentration.   What is
termed mechanical work, therefore, that is, work
that can be done without special thought or direction, can be carried on perfectly by the automatic
action of the subconscious while the conscious
mind may be thinking about something else.   But
it is not well to carry this practice too far.

To place certain kinds of simple work in the
hands of the subconscious while the conscious
mind is otherwise engaged may have a tendency
to separate the actions of the conscious and the
subconscious phases of mind; but this separation
must be avoided as it is perfect unity of action between the conscious and the subconscious that we
seek to attain, because when this unity becomes
perfect, the subconscious will always respond to
the directions of the conscious mind.   We have
discovered that the subconscious can do and will
do whatever it is properly impressed or directed
to do, but the conscious mind cannot direct the
subconscious properly unless there is perfect unity
of action between the two.

To think of something else while you are doing
mechanical work is permissible to a degree, but
it must not be made a general practice.   The
wisest course is to give your whole attention to

what you are doing now whatever that work may be; and if you give soul to that work it will cease to be mechanical.   Besides, such a work can be made a channel for a fuller and a larger expression of self.   All kinds of work may become channels of expression for the superior powers of mind and soul, and the secret is to give soul to everything that is being done.   To give soul to your work is to work in the conscious interest of what you are doing; in brief, to feel that your work is an expression of more and more life, and that expression will steadily increase the power of your entire mind and personality.   In other words, you give soul to your work when your whole heart is in your work; when you are thoroughly interested in the work itself and the final result; when you deeply love it and thoroughly enjoy it; and when you give it your very best thoughts, ability and power.   In this connection it is important to remember that what you give to your work you give to yourself.   The more ability and power you give to your work the more ability and power you develop in yourself.   And the more interest you take in your present work the better will your concentration become.   To take only a half hearted interest in what we may be doing now is to weaken the power of concentration; in fact, the power of concentration will almost disappear if such a practice is continued.

No one, therefore, can afford to be otherwise than thoroughly interested in the work of the present moment, no matter what the work may be. Occasionally, however, simple tasks may be left to automatic mental action; that is, when we have done those things so many times that their doing has become second nature, so to speak; and we may thus give our conscious attention at the time to other matters. But such a practice should be the exception, never the rule.

A fact of exceptional importance that we shall all discover as we apply the principle of concentration, is that no task can be disagreeable when approached in the attitude of real concentration. The reason why is found in the fact that when we concentrate properly we approach a subject or object from the most interesting point of view; and nothing can be really disagreeable when approached from the most interesting point of view. The value of this fact will increase as we realize the importance of avoiding every attitude of mind that is in any way antagonistic to our work. And as real concentration will perfect all such attitudes, we find what a gain we shall make in every respect when we learn to concentrate in the right way. We concentrate naturally upon that in which we are interested. For this reason the natural method for the development of concentration is always to look for the most interesting points of view; and we should apply this method, no matter what we may be thinking about or what our work may be. Everything has an interesting side, and when we look for it we shall invariably find it. In fact, to look for the interesting side will in itself create interest; and to create interest is to develop concentration. In this connection it is well to remember that no work can possibly be drudgery when entered into in the right frame of mind. And also that all work that is performed in the right frame of mind will open the way to something better. This is a law that never fails, and the right frame of mind in each case consists of the right use of concentration; that is, producing concentration by becoming deeply interested in what we may be thinking of or doing. In other words, to look for the most interesting points of view regardless of what conditions or circumstances may be.

IMPORTANT RULES.

1.—In all efforts to develop the brain through subjective concentration always concentrate upon the brain center first, and from that point gradually move attention to the outer surface.

2.—During concentration the mind should be in a well poised, serene attitude, and strongly determined to secure results.

3.—Fifteen or twenty minutes is long enough to practice at a time, and two or three times a day for regular exercise, although it is well to practice for a few minutes every hour if opportunities present themselves.

4.—Never concentrate for brain or mind development immediately after a meal. The digestive functions for about an hour after each meal require a full circulation and all available surplus energy. Therefore, neither the circulation nor additional energy should be drawn elsewhere at that time.

5.—The mind should continue in the attitude of perfect faith during the process of concentration. The more faith you have in the methods you employ the greater your results, because faith invariably awakens higher and more powerful forces.

6.—Affirmations, suggestions and strong positive statements may be combined with the process of concentration. To illustrate; while you are concentrating upon the faculty of intelligence, you may affirm, "My mind is clear, lucid and brilliant," "My mind is alive with exceptional intelligence," "My mind is constantly growing in the capacity to think, understand and create ideas," and statements of a similar nature. Statements to correspond with what you desire each faculty to become may be formulated by yourself, and affirmed as you concentrate for the development of that faculty.

7.—When concentrating, have superiority and worth constantly in mind, and train all the mental tendencies to move towards the higher and the greater.

8.—Never begin concentration until you have permeated the entire system with a refining process, and drawn all the forces of your system into finer states of life and action.

9.—While you are at your work, train your attention to act directly upon and through the faculty that you are using in your work. This will increase the power and the activity of that faculty, thereby developing the faculty at the time, as well as producing better work.

10. Never be over anxious about results, because you know that results must inevitably follow; then let results come when they are ready. If you proceed in this attitude you will begin to secure results from the very beginning.

11.—It is not always well to try to develop a number of leading talents at the same time. Select one or two that you expect to develop for your life work; then give these fully three-fourths of your attention, and divide the remainder of your time among all other faculties so as to produce a balanced mentality.

12.—It is not necessary to form any mental picture of the brain or the brain cells while you concentrate. In fact, it is best not to do this, as such a practice will tend to draw consciousness away from the subjective into the objective. Do not think of the physical brain itself or of the physical cells, but simply keep in mind those higher and greater qualities that you desire to develop. And hold your attention upon the interior subjective process that is promoting the development. Concentrate your attention upon that part of the brain that you desire to develop, but think only of the finer or metaphysical counterpart of your brain at the time. In other words, give your attention to the finer mental elements that permeate the physical brain. Thus you will awaken those energies and elements that alone have the power to produce the increase in talent and power you desire.

CHAPTER XI

DEVELOPMENT OF BUSINESS ABILITY

To become successful in the commercial world, that entire region marked "business ability" in Fig. V. should be developed. Concentrate subjectively upon this region for ten or fifteen minutes every morning before going to work, and repeat the concentration for a few minutes several times during the day. When you concentrate upon this region animate your concentration with a deep, strong desire to make this part of the brain larger, more powerful and more efficient. Be alive and enthusiastic during the concentration, but be fully poised and self-possessed, and positively expect results.

It will be noticed that that part of the brain marked "business ability" in Fig. V. includes the first four divisions as indicated in Fig. IV. Therefore in concentrating upon the region of "business ability" it will be well to take these four divisions separately at various times of the day. Take ten or fifteen minutes every day for the development of this region as a whole without any thought as to its divisions. Some time during the day give a few minutes to the practical brain; at another time during the same day give a few minutes to the mechanical brain and the executive brain. Give most of your atention, however, to that division that seems to be smaller or less efficient than the others.

The practical brain and the financial brain should receive the most thorough development when the individual is engaged in the general business field. But the mechanical brain should always be a close second, as the power to construct, build up, enlarge and develop is absolutely necessary in the working out of a successful business enterprise. When the management of an enterprise demands the greatest amount of attention, the executive brain should receive the most thorough development, while the practical brain should receive the first thought when the working out of details constitutes the principal line of action.

Speaking in general, the manager of an enterprise should constantly develop the executive brain; the general office force should constantly develop the practical brain, so that the ideas of the manager would be actually and efficiently carried out; the financial heads of the concern should constantly develop the financial brain, while every one connected with the enterprise should give daily attention to the entire region of "business ability." In addition to the development of gen-

FIG. V.

1. Business Ability
2. Construction and Imagination
3. Intuition

eral business ability, the man who would become a great power in the commercial world, should also develop "originality," the secret of greatness, and "intuition," or finer insight, the power to see through every circumstance and condition, and thus take advantage of the right opportunity at the right time.

Men and women who occupy stenographic or clerical positions should develop the practical brain in particular, and the entire region of "business ability" in general. Those who are employed in any form of constructive work should give special attention to the mechanical brain and the practical brain. If your clerical position is principally in connection with money, develop the practical brain and the financial brain. Foremen, superintendents and managers in factories should develop the executive brain and the mechanical brain; while those who manage financial institutions, or who superintend the selling of products, should develop the executive brain and the financial brain. The executive brain and the practical brain should be developed by those who manage the detail work of any business concern; and it must be remembered that those who manage or superintend, in any manner whatever, must also develop the volitional brain.

Whenever you concentrate subjectively upon any division of the brain, try to increase the active power of the faculty that functions through that part; and also try to improve the quality of that faculty. This is readily done by combining the proper desires and mental attitudes with the action of concentration. When you concentrate upon the practical brain, desire the power of practical application; think deeply of what it actually means to be practical, and try to evolve perfect system out of every group of thoughts, ideas or plans that may appear in your mind at the time.

When concentrating upon the mechanical brain, deeply desire to construct, invent and build up; try to put together the different parts of your business in every imaginable combination, and try to work out a combination that will be far superior to the present arrangement. You thus develop the constructive brain and the mental faculty of construction at the same time; besides, you may, at any time, invent a combination in your business affairs that will double your success.

When you concentrate upon the financial brain, desire wealth; desire a vast amount of legitimate wealth, and make up your mind to secure it; think deeply of that power in human action that accumulates, that gathers together, that produces increase, and try to feel that the power is becoming stronger and stronger in you. When concentrating upon the executive brain, think constantly of the practical art of management; examine the governing power from every point of view, and analyze as perfectly as possible that faculty in the human mind that is naturally adapted to manage, govern and rule. Deeply desire this faculty, this power, and inspire your desire to govern with the positive conviction that you can. In this manner you not only develop and enlarge the executive brain, but you also bring forth into practical action all the mental qualities that go to make up executive power. In consequence you will constantly gain greater and greater executive power; and if you continue in your development you will, in the course of a reasonable time, be able to manage successfully the most extensive enterprise in the world.

CHAPTER XII

ACCUMULATION AND INCREASE

The upper half of the brain is devoted to the abstract, to the world of ideas. The lower half of the brain is devoted to the concrete, to the world of things. And since the commercial world deals directly with the concrete, the lower half of the brain must necessarily be well developed if the increase of business ability is desired.

It is usually not difficult to formulate plausible theories concerning what ought to be done, but to apply such theories is quite a different matter; and application invariably demands the ability to apply in the world of things what has been worked out in the world of ideas. Most theories may be good, but not one in a hundred is ever applied, the reason being that there is a decided lack in the power of application among most minds. In the business world it is the man who can do things and who can put ideas into practice that is in the greatest demand. It is such a man who secures the best positions and a princely recompense; and on account of his exceptional worth he deserves all that he receives.

The man who can evolve system in his work, who can formulate methods for the more thorough application of his work, and who can practically apply for actual results all those methods, is never going to fail in his undertakings. And this proves that the power of application has such extreme value that even the man who has no other accomplishment can achieve great things in life if this particular power is highly developed. Though the power of application is of unusual value in every line of work, it has its greatest value in the business world, because in that world results cannot be secured unless the practical element is present in a large measure. The business man should therefore give a great deal of attention to the development of that part of the brain through which the faculty of application naturally functions.

When concentrating upon the faculty of application try to evolve system out of everything that you may be thinking of at the time. And this is very important as there must be system in all action before actual results can be secured. During such concentration, it is best to think principally of the work in which we are now engaged and try to perfect system in that work. In this manner you will apply your efforts in brain building more directly, and accordingly will develop your business ability to a much greater degree and in much less time.

The power of construction is absolutely necessary in the business world; therefore while concentrating for the development of constructive power, think deeply about your work and try to bring the different parts of your work into just such combinations as you desire. In brief, try to think out combinations that you feel will prove superior to every combination along constructive lines that you have worked out before. Thus you develop not only the brain in that particular region, but you also build up the corresponding faculty in the mind—that mental faculty that is applied in all constructive efforts.

You may not adopt all the new combinations that you will evolve in this manner, but you will develop the power of construction in your mind the more you try to evolve superior combinations; and through this practice you will finally evolve some exceptional combination from which the greater results you desire will be secured. It is a well known fact that success in the commercial world depends largely upon the way the business is constructed. Therefore, better and better results will inevitably follow as you increase your power to combine the various parts of your business in such a way as to give the entire enterprise, in which you are interested, the most perfect working system available.

In the world of things we find both the scattering process and the process of accumulation, and when we examine the subject closely we find that each individual has both of these processes in his own hands. He can control things to such an extent that he may positively determine how much is to be scattered in one place and how much is to be accumulated in some other place. In brief, he controls absolutely the disposal of all things and all possessions in his own world. In the majority, however, this faculty has not been developed, and for this reason we find only a small majority who are in possession of abundance, or who have the power to recuperate instantaneously should losses be incurred. But nature is able to give us abundance, and we all can secure abundance if we apply ourselves fully and in harmony with natural law. One of the most important essentials in this connection is the mental power of accumulation, for we must remember that we must be able to accumulate in the mind before we can accumulate in the external world. And as previously stated, this power can be increased more and more for an indefinite period through the proper development of the mind, and through the full development of that part of the brain through which this faculty functions.

To proceed, concentrate for the development of accumulation as outlined elsewhere in this study; and hold in your mind as clearly as possible the idea of accumulation at the time. Realize that you are an individual center, and that you can cause all the rich things in life to gravitate toward yourself as this center. Establish in your mind a deep feeling of what you imagine the process of accumulation to be, and try to feel that the various forces and elements in your system are actually accumulating within you. Hold yourself in a strong attitude of poise, and realize that through this attitude you are holding all things together in your system. Practice these things while concentrating until you realize your own supremacy over things, and feel distinctly the process of accumulation constantly at work in your entire system. The result will be a rapid and steady development of the power of accumulation, not only in your own mind, but in all those faculties whose function it is to gather abundance in the world of things.

It is a fact well known among all minds who have studied these deeper laws, that whenever you establish a certain process in your own system you can establish the same process in your environment. In other words, should you apply this law to the idea of accumulation we would find that you would have gained the power to accumulate possessions in your external world, when you have gained the power to accumulate the richer elements of your own mind. And experience proves that this law is absolutely true. Accordingly, we should seek to attain the consciousness of accumulation and create the accumulating process in our own mental world; that is, we should hold the mind in this consciousness while concentrating for the development of those faculties of the mind that are directly concerned with accumulation; and we will thereby, not only develop the brain in the region of those faculties, but will also develop the mental power to acquire and hold possessions both in the mental world and in the world of things.

CHAPTER XIII

INDIVIDUAL ADVANCEMENT

Progress and Success—The true meaning of success may be expressed in the one word "progress." You are successful only when you are moving forward, when you are constantly gaining ground in the most comprehensive sense of that term. Therefore, the first essential to those who have success as their goal, is to make individual progress their first and leading aim. And to this aim should be added the constant desire to find better and better methods through which individual progress may be gained.

The Right Vocation—To begin, select the right vocation. In making your selection follow your strongest ambition; that is, if you can do something in that particular field now. Though if this is not always possible, there is another way that may be entered upon temporarily. Accept the best opportunity that you can find under present conditions, and resolve to make good. Then, in the meantime, proceed to improve your whole mind. This will not only enable you to do better work where you are, but it will also make you more familiar with what ability and power you really possess. A great many young men are very ambitious along certain lines, and therefore imagine that their greatest success lies in those lines. But after their entire mentalities become fully alive, they discover that their strongest powers lie in an entirely different direction. Accordingly, their ambitions change; they find their first ambitions to be simply the result of surface action in the mind, while their new ambitions are the result of their real, inherent ability, now awakened to action.

Arouse the Whole Mind—The first ambitions of most young men are "false alarms," due to shallow mental actions produced by some external suggestions. The small boy who wants to be a street car motorman, because that particular work fascinates his boyish notion of responsibility and position, is an illustration. And though those young ideas usually pass away on short notice, still they are frequently followed by other ideas and ambitions equally false and superficial. The necessity, therefore, of waking up the whole mind in order to develop the true ambition and get the proper clue to the correct vocation in each case is most evident. When you accept the best opportunity you can now find, and proceed to develop your whole mind while working in that particular position, you will soon re-adjust your ambitions, if those ambitions happen to be "false alarms." But if your ambitions actually are genuine, proceeding directly and naturally from your greatest natural ability, the waking up of your whole mind will only tend to make those ambitions stronger and more persistent than ever before.

Your True Ambition—When you find a certain ambition becoming stronger and stronger the more you improve your mind, you may rest assured that that is your true ambition. And if you follow that ambition, you will enter your true vocation. But if you find your ambitions changing as you proceed to build up every part of your mind, you will find it advisable not to follow any special ambition, or select any special vocation until your whole mind is thoroughly aroused, and the strongest faculties determined with a certainty. Wherever you begin in your chosen vocation, you will find it absolutely necessary to promote your own individual progress if you wish to succeed. And by individual progress we mean the constant improvement of your whole self—your mind, your faculties, your powers, your character, your mode of thinking, your conduct, your disposition, your personal life, your personality, your power of application, your habits, your views of life, your personal worth, your ideals—in brief, everything that pertains to your own individual life, thought and action.

Individual Progress—If you are already in the right vocation, individual progress will enable you to meet the ever growing demands of that vocation. And here we must remember that the man who does not improve himself in this age is the man who will be left behind, and later placed "on the shelf." The man who is constantly improving himself will be wanted in the world of action as long as he lives, regardless of his age or the color of his hair. But self-improvement is no hardship; it is a pleasure; in fact, there are few things that help more to make life worth while. If you are not in the right vocation, individual progress will soon bring out the best that is in you, so that you will not only know where you belong, but will be competent to go to work where you belong. Then, if you continue this progress and self-improvement, you will constantly advance externally by noting a steady improvement in your conditions. Improve yourself, and your conditions will also improve. This is the law; and it cannot fail when systematically applied. Realize that individual progress must precede individual success, and that individual progress must continue if success is to be permanent. Work unceasingly for the progress and improvement of yourself. Make it a point to build yourself up; and never bring this building process to a standstill. If you are in an uncongenial position, do not try to get out at once; do not force yourself out; but proceed where you are to build yourself up, and improve yourself to such an extent that you become indispensable where you are. You will soon secure a better position, and you will become much stronger and more valuable, on account of the discipline gained by "holding out" under adversity.

Secret of Advancement—Make difficulties and obstacles serve the greater purpose you have in view, and they will, if you enter every position with a view of using the demands of that position for making your whole mind alive. But in this connection do not make the mistake that thousands have who have entered temporary positions. After entering those positions they have failed to improve themselves; instead, they have permitted their minds to retrograde, and therefore have either continued for life in those "temporary" positions, or have been pushed lower still. This accounts for the fact that so many capable and well educated men are now holding inferior positions. They took the best they could find in the beginning, but ignored the necessity of individual progress, and therefore had to continue where they began year after year until they finally gave up hope of ever getting anything better. The mistake of these men must be rigorously avoided at every turn, and every tendency to fall into a "rut" must be stamped out completely. Work for individual progress every minute, and no matter where or how you begin, you will steadily advance in the scale. New and better opportunities will come to you all along the line as you are prepared to accept them. You will prove the fact that better opportunities are always waiting for the better man, and that the better man is invariably the man who makes individual progress his first and greatest aim.

CHAPTER XIV

THE GENIUS OF INVENTION

There are few worlds that hold richer possibilities than the world of invention, and there are few things that are more easily developed than inventive genius. Everything can be improved. Even the most perfect products of the industrial world have defects, and the man whose genius can remove those defects will be most richly rewarded. In the world of new and original inventions there are no limitations whatever. The field is simply inexhaustible because there is no end to the realm of ideas, and invention is simply a new combination of ideas that can be turned to practical use. Another reason why the world of invention is so immense is because inventive genius is not confined to a single field of action. It is, on the contrary, employed in nearly every field of action. A certain grade of inventive genius is absolutely necessary to the writer; another grade is indispensable to the musical composer; still other grades are required by the artist, the mechanic and the skilled worker; while no business man will succeed to any extent unless he has the power of invention developed to a high degree.

The secret of inventive genius is the power to create new ideas, and to produce new combinations of ideas using both old ideas and new ideas as the case may require. The power to combine ideas for practical use is the most important phase in the development of inventive genius at the present time. There are innumerable ideas afloat in the world today that have not been turned to any account; even a few of these if properly combined, and practically applied would revolutionize the industrial world. It is, therefore, not necessary to search for new ideas at the present time while the world is waiting for a genius to tell us how to use the best ideas we already possess.

To proceed with the improvement of any invention a definite plan should be employed, but new inventions, new and original combinations frequently come of themselves while inventive genius is being developed; or they may come when the inventive genius, one may already possess, is aroused to an extraordinary degree by some powerful suggestion or experience that bears directly upon the necessary phases of mind. The first essential in the improvement of the invention is to gain a clear understanding of the principle upon which that invention is based, and the purpose which it is intended to fulfill. If the old invention does not fulfill that purpose with satisfaction, find the reason why. If your objective mind cannot give you your real reason, consult the subconscious. The subconscious can work out the most difficult problems in mathematics while you sleep; then why should it not be able to discover the real cause of imperfections in the invention you desire to improve, and also discover the key to the necessary improvements. The fact is that the subconscious can find out almost anything provided it is properly impressed and directed. And since we all can learn to direct the subconscious in any way desired, we should never permit ourselves to ever use the term impossible.

When you have found the cause of the imperfections of any invention, the proper combinations required to remove those imperfections can be easily made by applying the faculties of imagination and construction, though in this as well as in all other efforts, the subconscious should be brought into the fullest use possible. In its last analysis every improvement is the result of a better mental conception of the workings of the thing to be improved. Therefore, before undertaking to make the proposed improvement, the object under consideration should be analyzed from every possible point of view. In this connection it is highly important to know that there is nothing that will produce so many new combinations of ideas as the practice of looking at every object from every imaginable point of view; and this is especially true when we look at things with an interest that is deeply felt and thoroughly alive. The average person looks at things from a single point of view only; therefore his mental conceptions are one sided. His ideas are incomplete, and such ideas as are required to produce the new combinations or inventions desired are not forthcoming. Those necessary ideas, however, may be gained by taking new points of view, one after the other, until the object under consideration has been viewed and examined in every conceivable manner.

When you have examined something from every viewpoint, you have gained all the ideas of that something that your present mental capacity can comprehend. By combining those ideas, you will have a combination that must necessarily be an improvement upon that which you originally examined, and by turning this new combination to practical use you will have an actual improvement. The simple practice of looking at all things from every imaginable viewpoint will alone develop the power of invention to a remarkable degree, and when this practice is combined with a practical system of development in the art of invention, the attainment of real inventive genius is absolutely certain.

The principal faculties to develop in order to gain inventive genius are imagination, construction and intuition.   The latter may also be termed insight, discernment, or the power of discovery. To begin, concentrate upon those faculties twice every day, giving about ten minutes to each faculty, and while concentrating upon a certain faculty exercise that faculty in the work which it is being developed to perform.   To determine where to concentrate for the development of the brain in this connection see Figure VI.   To illustrate, when you concentrate upon that part of the brain through which the imaging faculty is expressed, use the imagination to the fullest extent and use it in picturing the various parts of the invention you desire to perfect.   This invention may be a book, a musical composition, a machine, an architectural structure or a group of plans and methods for the promotion of some commercial enterprise.   In other words, while you are concentrating upon that part of the brain which is used by the faculty in question, put that faculty to work.   You will thereby develop both the brain and the mind at the same time, which is highly important.

To develop the mental faculty alone is not sufficient.   You might just as well expect a great musician to do justice to himself on some crude, primitive instrument as to expect a highly developed faculty to express talent or genius through a crude sluggish brain.   For the same

FIG. VI.

1. Imagination   2. Construction.   3. Interior Sight

reason it is not sufficient to develop the brain alone. The brain is the instrument of the mental faculty; therefore when the faculty itself is not developed, there will be nothing in the mind to make full use of the highly developed brain that may have been secured. For this reason the faculty should be exercised whenever attention is concentrated upon that part of the brain through which the faculty naturally functions.

When exercising the imaging faculty during concentration the imagination should be used with some definite purpose in view. We should never permit the imagination to work at random, but should give it something special to work out into a complete mental picture. And here we should remember that the imagination is one of the greatest mental faculties in the mind. In fact, it is so important that no matter how practical or matter of fact your work may be, you will find it absolutely necessary to develop your imagination to the very highest degree if you wish to secure the best results obtainable through that particular work.

It is imagination that plans the greater enterprise and that supplies the necessary methods for successfully promoting that enterprise. Nothing great was ever done that was not first worked out in the imagination, and no improvement was ever made that was not first conceived and pictured in the imaging faculty. It is the power of imagination that lifts the products of mind above the crude and the ordinary, and that gives real worth to that which has worth. Everything that man has made was born of the imagination. And man has made some things that are truly marvelous, regardless of the fact that imagination has never been systematically cultivated. We can therefore imagine what we may expect when this remarkable faculty is thoroughly cultivated and highly developed.

When concentrating upon the faculty of construction, use that faculty in carrying on a definite building process in your mind, directing attention principally upon those ideas that you wish to combine with a view of procuring a new invention or a new system for practical application in your work. During concentration on this faculty, all the ideas, plans and systems imaginable, in connection with the subject under consideration, should be arranged and rearranged in every conceivable manner until the best arrangement or construction has been secured. This exercise, if practiced during the proper concentration upon the brain, will develop rapidly and thoroughly that faculty that produces new combinations of ideas, and that turns those combinations to practical use; that is, that faculty which can invent, or that is usually defined, when in its highest state of expression, as inventive genius.

When concentrating upon that part of the brain through which the faculty of intuition functions, we should exercise the faculty of insight and discovery, by trying to see through everything that has been brought before our attention. In brief, we should turn our attention upon the hidden parts of those phases of life and work in which we are directly interested, and try to discern the real nature of those parts. We may not discover anything of value at the time, and still we may; but the exercise will positively develop the faculty of insight; and if we continue this development, that faculty will finally discover something, something that may prove of exceptional value. In addition, we should give as much attention as possible to the development of that faculty that is defined as interior understanding, and especially if we desire to employ the power of invention in the fields of art, music or literature. Or, if we wish to devote our genius to mechanics or architecture, we should develop the mechanical brain in addition. While if we wish to apply ourselves principally in the commercial world, we should develop business ability in addition to the other faculties mentioned.

Another essential in the development of inventive genius is the fullest preservation and the proper direction of creative energy. Invention is naturally a creative process in all its phases, and therefore requires more creative energy than almost any other use of the mind. For this reason it is highly important that the faculties of invention be well supplied with such energy. To this end, the development of poise is indispensable, so that all waste of energy may be prevented. And at least fifty hours of sleep should be taken every week so that the subconscious may keep the system well charged with its various creative forces. Try to average from seven to eight hours of sleep in every twenty-four, but if this allowance should be cut short one night on account of important engagements, retire earlier the next night and make it up. This is a rule that should be kept as rigidly as possible, as it will not only aid decidedly in supplying the system with the necessary amount of creative energy, but it will also aid remarkably in preserving good health for mind and body. Lastly, learn to transmute all those energies in the system that are not required for the normal functions, and turn all of that extra energy into the faculties of invention. The more of this energy you can give to those faculties, the greater will be the creative power of your inventive genius, and the greater will be the inventions that will spring from your brain.

IMPORTANT FACTS.

When thought and attention are concentrated subjectively upon any group of cells in the brain, those cells will multiply in number, and there will be a decided increase in their efficiency and energy-producing capacity. Accordingly, that mental faculty that functions through those cells, will express greater power and a higher degree of ability. Any part of the brain can be developed to an exceptional degree by this method, but the concentration must be subjective; that is, it must be deep and alive, and must actually feel the real or inner power of its own action.

Every division of the brain is in two corresponding parts, one part appearing upon the right side of the brain and the other on the left; every group of brain cells on the right side has a corresponding group on the left side; therefore, in concentrating for brain development, give attention to both sides, first changing from one to the other, and later, as you become more proficient in the art of subjective concentration, give your attention to both sides at the same time. Always begin all concentration at the brain center, and move the action of your concentrated thought toward the surface of the brain, giving special attention to the cells on the surface, as these are the most important.

Whenever your ambition is aroused, concentrate the force of your ambition upon that part of the brain through which you must work to realize your ambition. That is, if you are ambitious to become a great financier, turn your attention upon the financial brain, or if you are ambitious to become a great inventor, turn your attention upon the mechanical brain and the imaging brain whenever you feel the power of ambition arising within you; or whatever you are ambitious to become, turn the force of your ambition directly upon that part of the brain that must be developed before your ambition can be made true. You thus develop the necessary faculty, and gain the power to do the very thing you desire to do.

To push the development of any one faculty, concentrate subjectively for ten minutes every hour on that part of the brain through which that particular faculty functions. But before you begin, always place your thought in the conscious feeling of the finer forces of your mind. When concentrating upon any part of the brain, picture in your imagination the faculty that functions through that part, and draw a mental picture of that faculty in the largest, highest and most perfect state of development that you can imagine. You thus impress superior mental development upon every brain cell, and gradually every cell will grow into the exact likeness of that superior development.

During subjective concentration the mind should be well poised, deeply calm, but strongly determined to secure results. Act in the feeling of unbounded faith, believe thoroughly and deeply in the process, and you will arouse those finer and greater forces in your system that can make the process a remarkable success. Ten to fifteen minutes is usually long enough for an exercise in brain development; but you may continue for twenty minutes if you feel that you are having exceptional results. Exercises may be taken every hour or two, but never directly after a meal, as a perfect digestion demands that your mind be perfectly quiet for at least an hour after partaking of food.

When you concentrate upon any part of the brain, use such good suggestions and affirmations as tend to work in harmony with the development you desire to promote. When you concentrate upon the region of intellect repeat mentally with enthusiastic conviction, "My mind is clear and lucid," "My mind is becoming more and more brilliant," "My mind is growing steadily and surely in the power of genuine understanding," "My intellectual capacity is constantly on the increase," "I am gaining the power to know, to discern, to comprehend and to realize every fact and every truth that I may desire." Formulate similar suggestions and affirmations as your needs may require, and try to feel that you are moving into those greater things that your affirmations tend to suggest. When you concentrate upon the volitional brain, use suggestions that suggest greater will-power, greater personal force and greater self-control. When you concentrate upon the practical brain use suggestions that suggest the increase of the power of application, the power that does things. In brief, whenever you concentrate use suggestions that will prompt your thought to work with the process of development. You thus cause all your forces to work together in promoting your purpose, and great results will invariably follow.

CHAPTER XV

THE MUSICAL PRODIGY

The Power of Music—In the promotion of human culture, refinement and a higher order of life, consciousness and thought, there is no power greater than that of music. It is therefore an art that should be cultivated universally and cultivated to the very highest possible degree. Though all music tends to elevate the mind, it is the music of quality that exercises the greatest power and the most permanent effect. But such music is not as abundant as we would like, the reason being that really great musicians are rare. The number of people who are studying music is very large and is constantly on the increase, but the majority of these are simply learning to apply what talent they already possess. They are not trying to develop talent of music itself. This, however, must be done if real musical genius is to be gained, although it is evident that in order to accomplish this we must have new and superior methods.

Use Plus Development—To learn how to use the talent you possess is one thing, but to develop that talent itself is quite another. The educa-

189

tional systems of today are concerned almost wholly with the former. But the coming systems must concern themselves also with the latter or the many opportunities for superior attainment now at hand will be lost. There are thousands of excellent minds that could develop rare genius if permitted. But most of the systems in vogue do not develop, their object being simply to train. To give these thousands an opportunity to get away from the routine of mere training, and to give expression to the genius that is within them is one of the aims of this study. Not that training is to be neglected, for thorough training is indispensable, but there must also be something more. We must not rest content with simply the training of our talents. We must also do something definite and effective to enlarge and constantly develop those talents.

Possibilities—To state that anyone who already has considerable musical talent could, through the proper system of development, become a musical prodigy may seem to be far beyond the realm of actual fact. Nevertheless, it is scientifically true. And it is also true that those who have no musical talent whatever, can, if they have a strong desire for musical development, become talented to a considerable degree. And here we must remember that the possibilities of the mind are both limitless and extraordinary, so that if these possibilities are given a fair chance to express themselves there is no reason whatever why genius should not positively appear.

The Three Factors—To develop the musical faculty, the three great factors in all development, the brain, the mind and the soul must receive thorough and scientific attention. The soul, however, should be given the first place, because in music, soul expression is indispensable to high quality. The best music becomes mechanical and, actually ceases to be real music, when the soul is neglected in its expression; and the soul is neglected in too many instances. We find that the lighter forms of music, that music that in itself appeals only to the superficial sentiments, actually becomes superior in its tenderness and sweetness when expressed through some one who has soul; and it is a well known fact that the sweetest music always comes from the sweetest souls, the reason for which will be readily understood.

Brain Development—It has been stated before, and deserves emphasis as well as repetition, that the brain must be thoroughly developed whatever the faculty may be that is to be expressed, because the brain is the instrument of the mind. To neglect the development of the brain is to remain in the ranks of inferiority, no matter how powerful or talented the mind may be; but as the development of the brain has been almost wholly neglected, we must proceed to give this matter most thorough and most enthusiastic attention. That part of the brain through which the musical faculty proper functions is indicated in Figure VII, and it is this region that needs development where musical genius is the object in view. To develop this part of the brain we should concentrate as before upon the brain center, so as to accumulate as much creative energy as possible at that important point; and while concentrating in this manner gently draw the finer forces from all parts of the system towards the brain center. In a few moments energy will flow to this point through all the nerves, because all the nerves meet at the brain center. All the brain convolutions also meet at the same point, and it is therefore the point of accumulation of energy as well as the point from which energy must be directed to that part of the brain that is to be developed.

Abundant Energy — The accumulation of energy at the brain center by this process will not deprive any part of the body of its necessary power, because far more energy is generated throughout the system than is ever used, and most of it is lost on account of never being taken up and applied in any way. There are various ways to prevent this waste or loss, but none of these methods will be of value unless the energy thus preserved is taken control of and practically applied in some part of mind or body. Since fully three-fourths of the energy generated in the average system is lost, we shall, by preventing this loss, secure more than enough for the most extensive system of development that we wish to apply, without depriving any part of the body of its necessary supply. We may proceed, therefore, according to the method indicated, and after a few moments of concentration upon the brain center cause abundant energy to accumulate at that point. This energy should be directed towards that part of the brain through which the musical faculty functions. The first step should be to direct this energy to the right side of the cranium; the second step to cause concentration to be returned to the brain center; the third step to direct this energy to the left side of the cranium; and the fourth step to concentrate upon the brain center again as before. These four steps may occupy one or two minutes each, and when taken, the same process may be repeated several times, and the whole exercise taken two or three times every day.

Exercises in Concentration—All exercises in concentration for brain development should be deeply serene and well poised, but should also be very strong. Force and intensity, however, must not be permitted, because such actions are disturbing, and disturbed actions always prevent growth. But so long as the mind is well poised, the concentration may be very strong and persistent without producing any discord whatever. In all these exercises, we should remember that the object is to produce more cells, smaller cells and finer cells in that part of the brain through which the faculty of music functions; and this is accomplished when the concentration is full, strong, well poised, harmonious and subjective, so that the finer creative energies are supplied in abundance. When taking lessons in music, the pupil should, during practice, concentrate attention as much as possible upon both sides of the forehead as indicated in the Figure. This will not only develop the faculty of music itself, but will also increase the activity of that faculty at the time, which will mean that better results will be secured in the study of music, and each lesson mastered in less time.

Undivided Attention—When the mind is concentrated upon these regions of the brain while you are taking lessons in music, or performing in music, the quality of the music you produce will be far better, though it may be argued that such concentration will divide attention, and take the mind off from the music in a measure. But this is not the case. When you concentrate upon the music you are producing, you should aim to cause

your mind to pass through that part of the brain,
so to speak, that is employed by the musical faculty. This can be accomplished with a little practice; and in a very short time the one mode of
concentration will keep your attention upon the
music as well as causing the activity of your mind
at the time to act directly upon the proper brain
regions as you perform.

Continuous Improvement—The great value of
this method is that it not only increases and im-
proves results in the person, but also develops the
musical talent itself, so that far greater results
may positively be secured in the future. This will
insure continuous improvement, and since the
possibilities of every talent are unlimited, there is
no end to what can be gained through that talent,
provided the methods necessary to continuous
development and improvement are constantly and
faithfully applied.

Feeling in Music—To secure more feeling in
your music give special attention to the development of the region of emotion as indicated in
Figure III. And this is most important because
the more real feeling you can give to your music,
the deeper will be the impression produced by your
music upon all minds that have the privilege
to be present when you perform. For this reason
every good musician must be highly developed in
the realms of emotion, although in this connection

it is necessary to cultivate a well balanced and well poised mind, so that those emotions are always under control, and always full and harmoniously expressed.

Appreciation of the Classical—When the faculty of interior understanding as indicated in Figure III is well developed, you will be able to appreciate classical music. Classical music is, strictly speaking, metaphysical music, and therefore appeals only to those minds that have become conscious of the deeper and the higher realms of thought. This does not mean, however, that those who appreciate classical music will necessarily appreciate the philosophy of metaphysics, as metaphysics is very large, and gives room for a thousand phases, and ten times as many more combinations; but the fact is that classical music comes directly from the realms of superiority and worth, and is therefore appreciated only by those minds that are conscious in a measure of superiority and worth. Such music also awakens in the minds of those who respond a still finer consciousness of the real quality of all things. During a classical performance you invariably withdraw from the superficial side of existence, and dwell more or less in the great depths of mind and soul. And the more highly you are developed in the broader metaphysical consciousness, the more real enjoyment you will secure from classical music. It is therefore well for everybody to enlarge the faculty of interior understanding, and it is absolutely necessary for those who wish to produce classical music. In this connection we must emphasize the fact that no one can become a genius in music without developing most thoroughly the faculty of interior understanding. And for this reason all such methods as have been given in previous lessons for the development of this faculty should be studied and applied with the greatest of care. When we examine classical music, we find that much of it is incomplete, due to the fact that interior consciousness or consciousness of high worth was not in full activity in the mind of the composer during every moment while the production was penned. When the great musicians of today, however, begin to give attention to this matter, and secure a higher state of interior understanding, we shall have classical compositions that will be far superior to anything that the masters of the past have produced.

Consciousness of Harmony—One of the first essentials to higher musical development in the musical world is the consciousness of harmony. The musician should not only live in perfect harmony, but should constantly seek to attain a deeper and a deeper realization of the very principles of harmony. And this being true, we realize that every musician who permits a single feeling of discord in mind or body, places thereby an obstacle in his way both with regard to the expression of music and the further development of the musical faculty. All real music contains the life of harmony to a greater or lesser extent; but how much of this harmony it contains will depend both upon the composition and upon the performer. A performer, however, who has found the world of harmony will express that lofty state even though the music may be lacking in a measure in this respect. To become a great musician, the mind must master the very life of music. To do this, the consciousness of this life must be secured, and it may be secured through the realization of higher and higher states of harmony. We conclude therefore that it is absolutely necessary to be in harmony with one's self, with everything and with everybody if high musical development is to be attained.

Principle of Music—Closely connected with the attitude of harmony is the understanding of the inner principle of music itself, and this is a great essential. But as it is a very deep study, the average mind will necessarily be slow in grasping its full meaning and import. In this connection daily efforts in trying to consciously comprehend music itself will prove of great value. And as such meditations can be enjoyed during spare moments, the results desired can be realized without loss of time. Another essential along this same line is to try to key the mind to finer vibrations of thought, feeling and consciousness. To accomplish this, the study of the law of vibration will be necessary, because it is only when we know the scale of vibrations that we develop the consciousness of grade and qualities. It is an immense field, however, and interesting and fascinating beyond the expectations of the most imaginative. But to those who cannot give the subject thorough attention at present, very good results will be secured by trying to concentrate the actions of the mind upon the highest and the finest grades of thought and feeling that can possibly be imagined. Subjective consciousness will help greatly and the practice of transmuting the finer energies will help still more, so that by combining all these various methods, even though to a slight degree, the mind will soon be keyed to much higher grades of quality and action than before.

To Secure Quality—To dwell constantly in the attitude of superiority and worth is extremely important, because to become a genius quality must be considered; and to secure quality the mind must create only such thoughts as are patterned after that which has quality. It is therefore necessary to hold attention upon the superior side of life, and to live in such close touch with the world of real worth that you can actually feel the superior taking possession of your system. In furthering these efforts, no superficial, common or ordinary states of mind must be permitted. The mind must never dwell on the empty side or on the surface of things, but must be trained to move constantly towards the depths and the heights of the superior within. In addition, it will be necessary to do everything possible to develop a beautiful character and a complete mind of the highest order.

The Soul of Music—As stated before, it is the soul that should receive the first attention in musical development; and by the soul we not only mean the real you, the individuality, but also everything within you that pertains to the lofty, the beautiful and the sublime. All those things that emanate from the ideal side, the finer side, the transcendental side in your life belong to the soul, and these things will give soul to everything you do, provided they are permitted to be expressed. To come into perfect touch with this finer side or those loftier things that we feel at times but cannot define or describe, is the purpose we have in view. It is these things, when expressed, that give soul to music, and it is such music that carries the mind away upon the wings of sublime ecstasy. When we hear such music existence is transformed, life becomes a dream of eternal bliss, and we find ourselves in a higher, more perfect and more beautiful world than we have ever known before. When we soar to those heights we ask for nothing more than simply to live. And the reason why is simple. We have found real life, and whenever we find real life it is sufficient simply to live. When we return to this world again we sometimes wonder if our experience was a mere vision, but we soon conclude that it was real. It must have been real, because we have been changed. We have been immersed, so to speak, in the crystal wonders of real life, and we are decidedly different. Something has been added to our minds, to our feelings and to our thought; and that something keeps watch so that we can never again go down completely to where we were before. There are many ways through which the mind can be awakened to the beauty and the real worth of life, and music that has soul is one of the highest and one of the best of these ways. It is the one way that can touch the greatest number. Therefore, to be able to give soul to your music will not only enable you to become greater in your chosen vocation, but also enable you to become a greater power for good, the equal of which may not be found anywhere.

The Soul In All Things—There are reasons why the soul should be given first place in musical development, and those who will bear this in mind will find their future study of music to be far more successful than it has been in the past. But in order that we may bring ourselves into more perfect touch with this finer something that we speak of as the soul of music, it is necessary to recognize and understand the soul in all things. There is nothing that will aid us more in the beginning along this line than to live in perfect tune with nature, and to try to listen constantly to the music of the spheres. Those who try to learn the spirit of nature's physical forms are usually looked upon by the practical as mere visionaries of no real value to the world, but history proves the fact that the creations of such minds are immortal. It is from such minds that the world has received everything that is worth while. We may, therefore, listen to the music of the spheres as much as we like. We may try to live more closely, and ever more closely, to the great spirit of nature, for nothing but good can come from such efforts; and when we employ wisely the inspiration thus received we shall give to the world real life. We shall create something that will never die. We shall write our own names upon the eternal rock of time, and beneath those names nature shall write genius, the highest title she can give to man.

Inspired Music—All real music is in a sense inspired, as it comes into mind when we are on the verge of the cosmic or in touch with the great soul of things. In brief, it is when we hear the symphonies of the vastness of the cosmos that we produce real music. When we hear real music we know where it came from, and we know that it came from the soul that was on the heights. We all long for such music principally because too much of the music we hear is simply "put together." It may pass away time pleasantly, but it does not open the heavens before us, nor awaken the spirit of man. If you would compose real music, therefore, live constantly on the verge of the cosmic. Thus you may do consciously and perfectly what the great souls of the past have done only in part. And here we should remember that there is such a thing as being touched by the spirit. The experience is real. It indicates that your mind is open to revelations, to higher and finer worlds; and this is

something that should be encouraged whenever possible, because it is the great secret, or
the open way, so to speak, through which man
receives everything that is lofty, marvelous,
wonderful or sublime. We have not considered these things in the past; but we must consider them now if we would give soul to all our
music, and develop our musical faculties to the
very highest states of real genius. For here
be it remembered that no music is true music
unless it has soul.

Soul Expression—Another essential is soul expression, or rather the living of the life of
music; that is, the giving of full expression to
that finer, higher something that may be de-
scribed as the music of human existence. The
importance of this will be realized when we
learn that the more soul we express in our living, the more soul we can give to whatever
may be expressed through us either in our
thought or in our work. To apply this idea
the musician should aim to give soul to
every note, and the more soul that is given
to every note, the more rapidly will the superior musical faculty develop. The inner
meaning of every tone should also be felt, and
that feeling should be expressed through every
vibration of the personality. Begin by attain-
ing as high and as perfect a consciousness of

FIG. VII.

1. Expression   3. Imagination   5. Memory
2. Tone   4. Intellect   6. Intuition

soul as you possibly can, and aim to express that soul whenever you perform or practice. You will soon discover the real meaning of it all; and when you do, you will know how to express consciously and perfectly the soul of every tone.   From that time on your music will begin to attain a quality it never had before.   Your progress will be rapid both in your power to perform and in the development of your musical talent.   You will not simply produce a succession of concordant sounds, but will begin to produce real music; and it is such music that the world wants.   Therefore, whoever can produce such music may look forward to a most brilliant future.

The Subconscious—To employ the best methods known for the training of the subconscious, will be found extremely valuable in musical development as well as in every other form of development.   To awaken the great within, and to train the subconscious to respond perfectly to the directions of the conscious—this is one of the greatest secrets in the development of genius along any line.   But before the increase of talent from within can be of real value, the brain and the mind must be made perfect channels of transmission and expression; and the soul must be called upon to give quality, superiority and high worth.

Leading Essentials—It is therefore necessary to give justice to all the factors involved, and to give special attention to those things that we may lack the most. The methods given for brain development are of special value; and as no practical system for brain development has been presented before, thorough attention must be given to this matter at once. To place the mind in a perfect and harmonious condition is an absolute necessity, because discord cannot produce harmony; and in music especially, harmony is the great principle. The soul must receive special attention, though in the development of that quality called "soul" we shall find it necessary to depend largely upon individual soul consciousness. Since the soul is beyond tangible rules no regular system of rules and methods can be given in this respect. But those who aim to realize higher and higher states of soul consciousness will soon secure the results desired. In addition, we should employ all the helps that we can find from every source, and to employ all these things as thoroughly and as perfectly as we can, for it is in this way that we shall reach the high goal we have in view.

The Spirit of Genius—The most important of all is to train both mind and personality to give full right of way to the spirit of genius, and especially when using the musical faculty in actual performance. Do not try to play or sing. Instead let the spirit of genius play; and let this same spirit sing. How it feels to be touched by the spirit of genius no one can describe, nor is it necessary. Those who will apply this system of development will soon feel this spirit themselves. Then they will know at first hand. They will also know how to give way to the spirit of genius, and give expression more and more to the musical prodigy of the great within. Then remember that there is something wonderful slumbering within you. That something can make you great. That something can make you a prodigy. That something, when fully awakened and fully trained for tangible action, can make you even a greater genius than the world has ever known.

CHAPTER XVI

TALENT AND GENIUS IN ART

In every vocation possibilities are both great and numerous when genius and talent are employed, and since we all can improve ourselves indefinitely, the greater possibilities of life may be realized more and more by everybody. For this reason no one should think that he must remain in a small insignificant world all his life simply because he is living in such a world now. In every field of action opportunities in an ever increasing number are at hand always waiting and watching to be accepted.

The idea that opportunities come but once is an idea without any foundation whatever, because the fact is that the opportunities that come into your life never take their departure. They continue to remain in a sense until they are accepted when they become a part of the life that receives them. Another fact of equal value is this, that the more opportunities we take advantage of, the more new opportunities we shall meet. It is therefore detrimental to our own interest to keep a single opportunity waiting. And there are many most excellent opportunities waiting for us all this moment, no matter what or where we may be. We shall find this to be absolutely true, because the more familiar we become with the subject the more convinced we become that the opportunities in one field are neither greater nor more numerous than in any other field. Therefore there is, strictly speaking, opportunity for all everywhere.

At present there are few worlds that hold so many opportunities for genius and talent as the world of art. And the reason is that the present age is nearer to the ideal than any other age in history. Thousands of people have recently entered that finer state of consciousness where they can appreciate real art, so therefore the time is ripe for the real artist. When we speak of the real artist, however, we do not mean someone who can simply paint well. Thousands can do that who have not the slightest genius for art. Something more is required besides the ability to place pictures on canvas for the work of the real artist is alive. It has character and soul and is not only a living thing now, but is immortal.

Too much of the good art with which we are familiar has very little character. It may be correct from an artistic standpoint and it may be beautiful. It may also be true to life; that is, true to the life that it pictures, but it does not always inspire that finer, higher something that makes man feel that he is more than a mortal creature.

This, however, real art can do and should do. But the artist himself must inwardly feel those higher qualities before he can express them in his pictures. In this connection we find that laxness whether in mind or character always appears in the product of the individual. When his genius lacks character his work also lacks character. His admirers may rave over his remarkable creations, but something is absent that ought to be there, and on account of that absence the creation fails in its real mission. This is also true in every other vocation. The mind that has both character and ability produces far greater and far more lasting results than the mind that has simply ability alone. It is therefore to everybody's advantage to develop character, no matter what their work may be, and this is especially true of the artist.

The work of the artist appeals to the finer elements in man, and when there is character combined with idealism in his work, the effect of his work will always be increased accordingly. Idealism without character has a tendency to produce idle dreaming, aimless imagination and various forms of sentimentalism that frequently react into morbid moods of depression. But when idealism and character combine, a constructive process begins in the mind, a process with a sound substantial foundation, and a goal as high as perfection itself. For this reason it is highly important to awaken in the mind those elements that tend to combine idealism and character. And there is no one that can awaken those elements to a higher degree than the real artist. And therefore the artist has it in his power to render exceptional service to the human race.

To become a real artist there are a number of faculties and qualities that should be developed, though the three greatest essentials are soul, character and the proper development of the brain. The artistic talents employ several parts of the brain, the first of which is form, or that part of the brain that extends from the brain center to the region between the eyes. The second is construction, occupying the region between the temples. When form and construction are well developed, the faculty of drawing will appear, but if there are no other artistic faculties in evidence this power to draw well will be simply mechanical, and will be of service to those who are employed in mechanics or architecture. The third brain faculty is the perception of color, and is found in or about that region that occupies the outer half of the eyebrow. The fourth is the imaging faculty located directly above construction. And the fifth is the perception of the ideal, the sublime and the beautiful, located directly back of the imaging faculty. To determine the exact location of these faculties see Figure VIII.

To concentrate subjectively upon these various parts of the brain, for three minutes several times every day will, in a few months, begin to show decided results in the development of artistic talent, although these results will be greater when the process of concentration is carried on in the proper mental attitudes. To illustrate, we should aim to analyze and measure shape and form with the mental vision whenever we concentrate upon the region of form; that is, we should take the three dimensions, length, breadth and height and mentally combine them in every shape and form imaginable. This will develop the mental shape of form as well as that part of the brain through which the faculty of form functions. When concentrating upon the region of construction, a similar mental process should be employed though with this difference, that more attention should be given to the size, the form and the shape of the structure in building; that is, instead of simply combining dimensions in the mind, we should try to build up or actually construct according to our highest ideal of form and construction. The faculty of form conceives the exact form and shape of every individual part, while the faculty of construction tries to take all these various parts and

FIG. VIII.

1. Expression of Form   4. Imagination
2. Perception of Color   5. Perception of The Beautiful
3. Construction   and Sublime

build them up into some definite and ideal structure.

When concentrating upon the faculty of color we should analyze with the mind all the colors that we know, and try to blend them mentally in every way imaginable. The mental experience that is enjoyed in connection with this practice is beautiful beyond description. During the practice color scenes and panoramas of color will frequently appear before the mental vision. And in many instances they will outrival in gorgeousness everything that the imagination has ever been able to picture. When concentrating upon the imaging faculty try to paint pictures in the mind. Proceed to paint imaginary pictures upon imaginary canvas, and try to make these pictures, not only original, but extraordinary. Do not copy in your imagination something that you have seen, but try to picture something that physical sight has never seen. This will not only develop the imaging faculty, but will also develop originality, which is the secret of greatness. When concentrating upon that faculty through which the beautiful is received, turn attention directly upon the ideal. Try to see and perceive the ideal of everything in your physical world as well as in your mental world. Think about the high, the lofty and the sublime, and try to actually enter into the world of sublimity and grandeur. Also awaken the life and power of aspiration, and try to gain the largest consciousness possible of everything that has real worth and high superiority.

In addition to the above faculties, we should also cultivate the faculties of love and emotion, because this will give sympathy, a quality that is absolutely necessary in all art. The real artist must be in sympathy with nature in general and with human nature in particular, though this sympathy should always seek the finer touch of the more beautiful side of everything. We should never sympathize with the undeveloped conditions of nature nor with the weakness of man; that is, we should not enter into mental contact with those things nor imitate mentally those conditions. Such a sympathy is always unhealthful; and unhealthful states of mind are not conducive to genius. It is not the shortcomings of nature nor the crude side of man that you are to love and admire, but it is the unbounded possibilities that we have the power to unfold and develop that we should select as our ideals, not only in art, but in living.

To understand the laws of harmony and gradation is indispensable to the artist. In addition to what is already being taught on these subjects in art schools, the development of mental harmony should be sought most earnestly. The real artist must convey the spirit of real harmony, and to give this quality to his art he must be conscious of the deeper harmonies of the soul. To this end, therefore, he should seek higher consciousness; that is, that consciousness which reveals the beauty, the serenity and the soul of all things. When a work of art has soul it will forever remain an inspiration, and that which inspires has the power to elevate man to higher states of living. In this connection we should remember that everything we see has a tendency to impress the mind. As these impressions are so are our thoughts, and as our thinking is so are we. Therefore, if we wish to become more than we are, and rise to the subconscious states of a better and a more beautiful life, we should surround ourselves as much as possible with those things that have the power to inspire; and there is nothing that will serve this purpose to a greater degree than works of art that have soul.

Whatever we may be doing, if we feel the soul at the time, we give soul to that which we do; and our work will therefore be classed with that which is superior. In the development of genius, however, many conclude that genius alone is sufficient to produce great ability and promote great achievements. But we have already discovered that this mysterious something that we call soul is just as necessary as genius itself, and in fact must be present before genius becomes real genius. Genius not only does its best work

through the avenues of virtue, truth, lofty mind-
edness and high spiritual qualities, but what is
more, genius cannot do itself justice unless those
qualities are present to a very high degree. In
other words, genius is not genius unless it has
soul and character; for without soul and character, genius is but a cheap imitation of its great
and wonderful self.

Another essential in the development of
ability and genius in art, as well as in the development of all other forms of ability, is to educate the subconscious along proper lines. The
subconscious can do anything if properly impressed. This is the law. Therefore the subconscious has the power to bring forth everything that is required for the faculties of art.
From this statement we are not to conclude, however, that the direction of the subconscious is all
that is necessary. To awaken the subconscious
is one essential and an essential that is indispensable, but to train the objective and develop the
brain so that the greater subconscious powers can
find orderly expression are other essentials
equally important. To impress the subconscious
along artistic lines, realize clearly in mind what
constitutes artistic talent; gain a perfect consciousness of art itself, and try to understand the
artistic spirit. In other words, form definite
ideas of art and of the art of which you wish to

become a master. Then impress those ideas upon your subconscious mind many times every day, being convinced at the time that what you impress upon the subconscious the subconscious will later on express in your mind and faculties. What we give to the subconscious will be returned to us in thirty, sixty or an hundred fold. Therefore, we must impress upon the subconscious the real ideas of art; and when we do we shall receive that power and genius in return that will give us great and even extraordinary talents in the wonderful world of real art.

CHAPTER XVII

TALENT AND GENIUS IN LITERATURE

The faculties required for literary work depend largely upon the field selected although there are a few faculties that all writers need in common. These are expression, construction and a highly active imaginative intellect. Where there is a desire to write on metaphysical or psychological subjects, interior understanding should be developed in addition to the ones mentioned. And to write well on scientific and practical subjects a thorough development of application is required because this gives one ability to connect principles and laws with the practical world. It also gives system, method and the faculty of turning the abstract into actual use. To become a good writer of fiction, develop the faculties of expression, intellect, intuition, emotion and originality. To these should be added what might be called universal consciousness, or the power to sympathize and enter into harmony with all phases of life.

In this connection it is important to mention that there are several new fields—fields that hold excellent possibilities for those who will prepare themselves for such a work. Ordinary fiction pic-

tures life as it is lived by human nature in its
weakness.   It is true to life as it is lived by those
who really do not know how to live.   Therefore,
it is largely a picture of flaws, perversions and
mistakes.   People read such fiction usually for no
other reason than to pass time or to be entertained,
although a great deal of fiction is read through a
morbid desire to devour what is hardly wholesome.   It is therefore evident that very little
good can come from the reading of ordinary fiction, and to be just to ourselves we cannot afford
to do what does not bring good in some way.   In
addition to the usual fiction we have fiction that is
out of the ordinary; that is, that constitutes superior and real literature.   Such fiction is highly
valuable for the richness of its language, and no
one can read such fiction without being decidedly
benefited along the lines of higher literature;
but such fiction does not as a rule contain anything of direct value concerning the secret of life.
Many will contend that it is not the purpose of
fiction to teach anything.   But the fact is that
there is no class of literature that could teach
the secrets of life in a more thorough and more
convincing manner than fiction.   Therefore, fiction that does not aim to be constructive as well as
entertaining ignores its greatest opportunity.

   To define the new fiction is hardly possible in
a brief paragraph, but its object is to picture life

as it might be lived by people who have mastered or are trying to master the secrets of life. In other words, it would not deal with ordinary people and their modes of living, but it would deal with the life and the conduct of such people as have taken it upon themselves to attain and achieve the greatest and the highest things that are possible in life. That such fiction could be made more interesting and more fascinating than anything that has ever appeared in print is evident, and if produced by a master mind would constitute a higher form of literature than has ever appeared in the world. The time is now ripe for such fiction, and to those who can produce it, fame and fortune in a large measure are surely in store.

To develop literary genius, the first essential is to develop those faculties of the brain and the mind that are required for such work. These faculties are indicated in Figure IX and full instruction as to their development has been presented in previous chapters. The second essential is to educate the subconscious along literary lines. This is extremely important, because there are few talents that respond as readily to subconscious training as the literary talent. Besides, it is in the subconscious alone that we can find real genius along any line. In the subconscious we find the limitless state of every faculty, talent or power; and we can steadily bring into expression more and more of this capacity, as no limit has been found to its power or possibilities. The real secret of becoming a genius is to awaken and properly train the subconscious mind, though we must not forget that the objective mind and the physical brain must be cultivated in such a way that subconscious genius can find full expression. To bring out the literary genius that may be latent in the subconscious is a process that cannot be perfected in a few weeks, but those who have considerable literary talent may, in a few weeks, realize a remarkable improvement from the application of right methods; and if they will continue indefinitely in the application of these methods, continuous advancement will positively be the result.

Those who may not be talented along literary lines, but who desire to develop such talents, can make their desires true to a very great extent if they will persevere for a year or more in the application of the two essentials mentioned. In this connection it must be remembered that the subconscious contains all the talents in a potential state, and it is our privilege to choose which one we desire to express, develop and apply. If that talent is already expressing itself in a measure it will take less time to increase its subconscious power, but if time, perseverance and the right efforts are combined, any talent desired can be developed to a remarkable degree, whether we have much ability along that line or not at the present time.

The first step is to gain a clear mental conception of what you desire to develop; and this desire should be full and strong at all times, as the subconscious will never respond to half-hearted desires nor divided attentions. When the desired purpose has been clearly pictured in mind, the next essential is to impress this with deep feeling upon every thought. Every thought which has deep feeling enters the subconscious and carries into the subconscious the desire with which it was impressed. As previously stated, the subconscious must be expressed in the present tense; therefore, do not simply desire to become a genius, but desire to bring forth the genius that already exists in the depths of your mind. Never impress the subconscious with the idea that you hope to become this or that. On the contrary, live in the strong, deep conviction that you have those things now, and this is true. A genius is asleep in the subconscious of every mind, and the subconscious is a part of you. It belongs to you. Therefore, you possess now all that is in the subconscious. For this reason it is strictly scientific and absolutely correct to affirm positively that you now have, and that you now are, what you wish to possess or become.

Live in the conviction that you already are a literary genius. Know that it is true, and stamp that conviction upon every thought you think. If necessary use affirmations to establish that conviction. It is always well to use affirmations provided we feel the real truth that is contained in all such statements. These affirmations may be made at any time, but they should without fail be impressed upon the subconscious every night before going to sleep. Take fifteen or twenty minutes every night after you have retired, and impress deep, positive statements upon the subconscious, affirming such ideas as you wish the subconscious to perpetrate and develop. Then go to sleep with the conviction that you now are a literary genius. Statements like these may be employed: "I am a literary genius;" "I am a brilliant writer;" "I have strong, clear, lucid mind." "My literary ability is unbounded, and of the highest order;" "I am complete master of the richness of language;" "I have at my command innumerable ideas;" "I am original in thought and in expression;" "Well constructed expressions are always ready to flow through my mind;" "I am alive with my subject and can give it the fullest, the freest and the most perfect expression."

Many other statements of a similar nature can be formulated and employed, though it is not well to use too many. The object is to carry into the depths of the subconscious the idea that there is genius within you, and that this genius is now ready to express itself in rare literary ability. While affirming these statements your attention should be concentrated upon the subconscious side of those parts of the brain that are employed in literary work. Then expect results now; and persevere until results do come, never permitting yourself to become discouraged in the least even though you have to work for months before you secure the desired subconscious response. Through perseverance and the right methods, results positively will come; and when they do come, you will be on the way to a development that will certainly mean much for the future.

CONCLUSION

VITAL ESSENTIALS IN BRAIN BUILDING

Moments of Tranquility—In all growth the passive is just as necessary as the active. Moments of action must invariably be followed by moments of repose, and the mode of repose should be selected with the same scientific care as the mode of action. To know how to properly apply a faculty is highly important when certain results are held in view, but it is equally important to know how to rest, relax and amuse that faculty in order to secure those same results. The reposeful attitudes accumulate; the active attitudes take up the new mental material thus secured, and proceed to build more largely. But the amount accumulated during any moment of repose is always larger when the mind expects accumulation during that moment.

When to be Still—Immediately following any form of positive action, physical or mental, the mind should be perfectly still for a few moments. Whether the action be actual work or simply exercise, the same rule should be observed. And also certain periods of tranquility should be taken at frequent intervals, varying from a few moments to a few days, depending upon the circumstances involved. The general purpose of such periods would be rest, recuperation and accumulation; and these are just as necessary to progress, growth or advancement as the periods of exercise, work and action. It is the moments of repose that give the moments of action the necessary material with which to work. This is a law that must receive constant and judicious attention wherever scientific attempts are made in the development of ability, talent and genius.

Relaxation—Any action of the mind tends to produce what may be termed the "keyed up" attitude, and this attitude is necessary to the highest state of efficiency. When you are "keyed up," all your faculties are at their best; they are fully aroused, thoroughly alive and are worked up to the most perfect point of practical ability. But when you are through with your work, the "keyed up" attitude should be discontinued for the time being. The majority, however, fail to do this; they sometimes continue in the "keyed up" attitude for hours after they have ceased to work; they even go to sleep in the same attitude, and then wonder why they do not sleep well, why they tire so easily or why their systems are almost constantly on the verge of breakdown. The attitude for work is for work only; when the work is done enter the attitude that is not for work; that is, relax, and give the system the needed opportunity to place itself in proper condition for the next day's work. To relax the system, breath deeply, easily and quietly, and think of your thought as going towards the feet every time you exhale.

Restful Harmony—The attitude of restful harmony should be entered at frequent intervals every day. A moment or two in this attitude is often the means of doubling the working capacity of the mind for the next hour. The restful attitude accumulates energy, while the harmonious attitude tends to place this new energy in the proper position for efficient action. Harmony always tends to set things right; therefore, the value of combining the feeling of harmony with the attitude of rest, repose or relaxation is readily appreciated. A few moments of restful harmony are especially important immediately after some exercise in brain building or mental development.

Recreation—What kind of recreation to select depends entirely upon your work. The two should always be opposites in nature, tendency and effect. If you are engaged in heavy mental work, choose recreation and amusement that is light, bright and sprightly. But if your work requires but little mental energy, choose recreation that tends to arouse mental energy. A stirring drama would prove highly beneficial to a mind that had been practically a blank during the day; in fact, such recreation might in time arouse enough mental energy to take him into some position where he could apply the full capacity of his mind. To a mind, however, that had been dealing all day with profound problems, a different form of amusement would be required. If you are stirred up continually by your work, do not select forms of recreation that have the same effect. Hundreds do this; they are in the midst of excitement all day in business; at night they choose some form of amusement that has the same exciting effect. In consequence, life is cut short a half a century or more too soon. Whether in amusement, entertainment, outdoor sports or reading for recreation, aim to select something that produces an effect directly opposite to that produced by your work. Through this practice you will do far better work, and you may add a quarter of a century or more to your life.

Diversion in Concentration—The actions of concentration will be thoroughly effective only when alternated with passive diversions. Concentrate regularly upon your leading purpose, and when you do concentrate, give the subject at hand your undivided attention; but have several interesting diversions to which you can give your passive attention at frequent intervals. To live exclusively for one thing is not to succeed in the largest sense of that term; nor can any mode of concentration produce the results desired unless it is placed at rest occasionally, and the actions of the mind turned, for the time being, in other directions. To cease action in a given line, it is necessary to promote action in a different line; therefore, diversions are necessary. And every action must cease at intervals in order to give that which is acted upon the opportunity to adjust itself to the results of that action.

Imagination in Repose—During moments of repose and relaxation the imagination should be directed to give its attention to that which is quiet and serene. When you are resting the mind, picture scenes of tranquility, and try to enter into that restfulness that such scenes will naturally suggest. The imaging faculty is never completely inactive. So long as you live you will think, and so long as you think you will imagine. Therefore, during serene moments, imagine the serene, and you will give perfect repose to your entire system. The power of the imagination is used extensively in the development of talent and ability; in fact, no development can possibly take place unless imagination is properly incorporated in the process. It is therefore evident that those moments of complete relaxation that should always follow every exercise for development must, to actually produce relaxation, direct the imagination to picture that which is in perfect repose. To relax mind and body is not possible so long as the imagination is picturing something that is not in repose.

Soul Serenity—This is that deeper feeling of calmness and peace that tends to tranquilize the finer forces and the undercurrents of the system. And this is very important, as it is this deep, interior state of poise that makes man a power. Soul serenity should be entered into several times every day; and the result will be that those mental forces that have been aroused through positive exercise in development will become more deeply established in the subconsciousness of the mind. That is, the result of every exercise will take root; it will find deep soil, and will live and grow as a permanent factor in the continual upbuilding of the mind.

Sleep—The mind should be deeply impressed, before going to sleep, with that degree of development that is desired; but before sleep is actually entered, every faculty should be placed in a state of perfect calm. To go to sleep properly is just as important in any form of mental development as any exercise we may take when awake for the promotion of that development. But all that is necessary in securing these results is to think deeply with a strong desire for the development we have in view, and calm the entire mind as we go to sleep. To accomplish this, simply relax, using the method for producing relaxation as stated above.

Recuperative Thinking—During moments of rest and repose, do not think of doing things, but think of enjoying things. The man who is always thinking of doing things may produce the quantity for a time, but the time will be short, and the quality will be absent entirely. The best results are always secured when thoughts of doing things are frequently alternated with thoughts of enjoying things. The simplest, the easiest and the quickest way to recuperate the mind is to think of enjoying things. A few moments of such thoughts are usually sufficient to restore full mental vigor; but those moments must be given over completely to thoughts of enjoyment; the doing of things must be wholly forgotten for the time being, and the mind must give its all to the pleasing picture it has elected to entertain.

Meditation—The practice of tranquil meditation is absolutely necessary in every form of mental development. It is a practice, however, that is rare, and this accounts for the fact that deep, profound, substantial minds are also rare. The many have not discovered the real riches of their own mental domains, and the reason is they have neglected meditation. The purpose of meditation is to "turn over" in the mind every idea that we know we possess.   We thus gain new viewpoints, and, in turn, new ideas.   Through meditation we become acquainted with the wonderful that is within us.   We discover what we are, what we possess, and what we may attempt. When we meditate we take a peaceful tour of investigation through the many realms of our own mind; we are thus brought face to face with many things that are new, and the tour will prove both a recreation and an education.   It is always a diversion, and it will never fail to entertain. Meditation will also properly place every new impression that has been received; thus it becomes a building process in the mind, and a factor of absolute necessity.   To practice meditation regularly is to become more and more resourceful, because meditation invariably gives depth to every phase of the mind.   The mind that meditates frequently does not live simply on the surface any more; such a mind is daily becoming enriched with the gold mines of the great within, and is gaining possession of larger and larger interior domains.   In consequence it finds more and more upon which to draw, and it will never be at a loss, no matter what the needs or the circumstances may be.

Rest—To give any part of the system rest, we must withdraw attention from that part, and to withdraw attention from any special part we must give the whole of attention to some other part. When the mind needs rest, exercise the body. When the body needs rest, read something of real interest, or listen to soothing music, or think of something that takes attention away from physical existence. Give proper rest to the body, and you will never lose your vitality, your virility or your vigor. Give proper rest to the brain and the mind, and you will never lose your brilliancy no matter how long you may live. But real rest for any special part is not secured by simply trying to cease action. You cease action in one part by becoming vitally interested in some other part. People wear out simply because they do not know how to rest. They are partly active in every part of the system continually. By becoming wholly active in a certain part, you become wholly inactive in all the other parts; and the inactive parts are perfectly rested. Then change about, regularly, giving each part of the system perfect rest for some moments several times every day. This is the art of resting; and he who rests well will work well and live well; he will also live long and do much that is truly worth while.

Printed in the United States
87871LV00013B/7/A

9 780766 178311